CW01500197

ISBN: eBook 978-1-0685754-3-3

ISBN: Paperback 978-1-0685754-2-6

ISBN: Hardcover 978-1-0685754-4-0

Practice eBooks® An imprint of Spiers Psychology Ltd. Wakefield, UK.

The following original text combines personal reflections, clinical observations, and fictionalised narratives. Where personal experiences are recounted, they are based on the author's own personal life or used with the full and informed consent of those involved.

Any identifiable details of therapists or other individuals have been changed or removed to protect privacy. All other characters portrayed in clinical settings, scenarios, and depictions are entirely fictional to protect client confidentiality. While based on common themes, any resemblance to actual persons, living or deceased, is purely coincidental.

The curious paradox is that when I accept myself just as I am, then I can change.

Carl Rogers – *On Becoming a Person* (1961)

Contents

Prologue   XI

1. Checking Boxes   1

2. Touching Stones   20

3. Adolescence   38

4. Thought Crimes   57

5. Original Sins   77

6. Echo's Chamber   97

7. Avoiding Cracks   116

8. Warheads   136

9. Containment   155

10. Unusual Suspects   172

11. New Blood   189

12. Precious Things   208

13. Drawing Circles   226

14. Leveraging Life   243

Before you go....   259

Endnotes   261

About the Author   279

Prologue

It was a crisp morning in early March of 2012. The hard frost overnight had covered the parking bay. I was reversing back and forth with the car door propped open, struggling to see whether I was between the faint white lines. There had been more traffic than anticipated on the run into town, and I was getting close to being late. The dump of adrenaline was sending my heart rate through the roof. I was becoming increasingly stressed and frustrated.

On the very cusp of slamming the car door shut and driving off, I would still be charged for the session. It would also be a bad first impression.

Hi Gill, sorry for the late notice. The lines in your car park are insufficiently visible. I couldn't park in a way that felt correct, so I drove home, having an epic tantrum like a six-year-old. I hope to see you next week, weather permitting. James.

After a lot of swearing and door handle checking, I pressed the key fob for the fourth time, just in case the car had magically opened in the last twenty seconds—then hurried to the door.

Gill was a cognitive behavioural therapist, and this was my third attempt at psychological therapy. I was in the process of selling my first business and preparing to start a university degree. Under the false impression that the lived experience of mental health issues would harm my career prospects, I sought a private therapist so it wouldn't show on my NHS medical records.

While I've experienced a range of intrusive thoughts over the years, with many compulsions since my early teens, health-related themes were the most common and arguably the most difficult to manage. Health anxiety can often present somewhere between generalised anxiety (excessive worry) and obsessive-compulsive disorder (OCD); mine have always been catastrophic movie-type intrusive thoughts about death and terminal illness. Whether about me, family members, or my dogs, it was generally most active during increased stress or transition periods.

My compulsions have ranged from habitual checking of my body, being on speed dial to the vet, to neutralise persisting fears of my dogs dying in the house while I was out at work. Also, gas poisoning, house fires and the dogs being stolen or killed on the road due to me accidentally leaving the door open. I would repeatedly press light switches and relentlessly check the oven and gas hobs, electrical sockets, doors, windows, and water taps to reduce anxiety around the thoughts.

Although I've been able to reasonably manage OCD over recent years, it has been costly in the past. Not just in terms of my well-being, but it has also impacted my relationships, causing rows and arguments over my need to perform ritual checks of the entire house before leaving to go anywhere. Inevitably, shouting at someone with OCD in the middle of their compulsions, interfering, or entering a room that has been checked will often serve only to contaminate the whole process, meaning that you have to start from scratch. Needless to say, it has caused issues over the years.

Then there's the financial costs. Aside from the nearly one hundred weekly sessions of private therapy, I've broken every door handle and window lock in the house and thrown away mountains of food because I decided it had an odd look about it, despite being in date. Yet, none of it has ever added up logically. Being able to leave the television plugged in, but not the kettle. Leaving the fridge plugged in but not the computer. Taking photos to ensure that things are properly switched off, despite knowing that photos cannot prevent an electrical fire or gas leak if there is an actual fault.

The first therapist I saw when I was diagnosed with OCD at the age of sixteen was a counsellor at my local GP surgery. Typical of teenagers, I didn't speak much. All I remember was that the therapist kept asking me if I loved my parents. He was getting increasingly frustrated with the monosyllabic response. Eventually, he gave me a metaphor for traffic lights and discharged me. Whenever I felt anxious, I was to imagine a red traffic light, then move to amber, then green, all while trying to slow my breathing down.

Safe to say, it did little to curb the intrusive thoughts that developed over the next two years: graphic images of pushing people under trains while waiting on the platform, repeatedly monitoring my vision for signs of a brain tumour, or the urge to crash my car into a tree, once I passed my driving test. And, while having never been suicidal, I spent several months during my early twenties avoiding bridges and multi-storey car parks on the off chance that I might give in to the strange urge to throw myself off the side.

I entered therapy again during my late twenties through the NHS, having around ten sessions. Once again, mostly calming exercises, the *STOPP* technique, similar to the traffic lights, and worksheets telling me that my thoughts were not facts. None of it touched the sides, but as can be common with perfectionists, I told the therapist it was all marvellous and tremendously helpful. I attended every session with a completed homework sheet, all embellished and written out the night before. I wrote them off as pointless, having tried the techniques only once.

Two decades later, and now a qualified psychologist, I understand that my lack of engagement with the process was partly to blame. Yet, both instances of therapy were focused on the management of generalised anxiety (worry): reassurance seeking and tolerance of uncertainty, as opposed to intervention specifically targeting obsession and compulsion. I also didn't fully understand where I was getting in my own way.

My experience with Gill would be different, to a degree. Although I didn't necessarily appreciate it then, she was absolutely on the ball regarding formulation and intervention.

+ ✳ +

Sitting next to the window, I realised her room looked out onto the car park. The frost had started to clear in the morning sun, and I could see that I was parked across two spaces, with the white line demarcating the bay running directly underneath the middle of the car. My internal critic starts barking at me. "How the hell did you pass your driving test?" I glanced to the left; I could see a car parked at an odd angle with the bonnet protruding from the space.

My external critic piped up. "What careless and thoughtless person leaves their car abandoned like that? No wonder I couldn't park straight!" Gill noticed me glancing at the car.

[Gill] Oh, that's mine; I couldn't see the line this morning either. Don't worry; the car park is private, and there are always spaces.

[Me] The lines are very faint.

[Gill] They are. Do you struggle when things don't go your way in other aspects of your life?

She was very direct—I liked that about her.

I'm embarrassed that she had seen my morning antics from the window, though. I felt angry and a bit upset. It was the first time in my adult life that anyone had asked me that question. I didn't know why it struck a chord, but it did. I had done a lot of research on OCD over the years, but had never paid much attention to my other quirks.

We began piecing things together over the first few sessions, starting with the A5 writing pad resting on her lap. By session three, Gill was stretching across a corporate-sized presentation board. The competing schemas of chaos and order are laid out in neatly drawn boxes, circles and arrows, like a map of the London underground. A combination of hypercritical, rigid and unrelenting standards and a healthy side plate of fearing harm and illness. I was officially knighted as a truly compulsive and obsessive person.

And, like many people with similar schemas, the only problem I could see from my perspective was the cycle of distressing, intrusive thoughts and relentless checking.

Gill was an experienced and intuitive therapist who helped me make sense of things. She recommended a combined treatment approach involving in vivo (with the therapist) exposure tasks to the most feared outcome of my thoughts. This involved digitally recording my imagined demise from a terminal brain tumour right up to the point of my funeral. My homework task was to repeat the exposure by listening to the recording at regular intervals during the week without engaging with compulsions. Commonly known in therapy circles as exposure and response prevention (ERP).

She also recommended combining this with eye movement desensitisation and reprocessing (EMDR). This was not typically offered on the NHS for OCD, given the evidence base being mostly anecdotal outside of treatment for post-traumatic stress disorder (PTSD). Still, she had seen better results with her previous patients when combining the treatment approaches.

True to my well-established patterns, I told Gill that this all sounded great and that I could understand her rationale. What I didn't tell her was that I knew I was not symptomatic of PTSD, and from what I had read online, ERP was the *gold standard*; it had a well-established evidence base. I wanted that—thank you!

In retrospect, I wish I had listened to her, but at the time, I was still under the false belief that I always knew best.

I recorded the exposure tasks during our sessions while maintaining emotional detachment and making intellectual connections. I would play the recordings during the week on loudspeaker while searching for support worker roles to keep me financially afloat while studying. I rationalised that I was too busy to take the time out. Although technically distracted, I wasn't engaging in my usual compulsions.

That was okay, though?

Obviously not!

Eventually, I started my university course and combined with a part-time job and lack of affordability due to the significant drop in income, I ended treatment abruptly. I sent Gill an email, telling her how much better I felt and that her approach was life-changing. I'm pretty sure she saw through it.

So why am I telling you all this? More to the point, why did I decide to write a whole book about it?

As you have likely gathered by this point, obsession and compulsion have been part of my life for as long as I can remember and also involve a large part of my clinical work.

Following a significant career change in 2012, I began the long and uncertain path into applied psychology training. I started treating people with OCD clinically in 2016. Initially at a low intensity, before moving into specialist psychotherapy as my career developed.

I also have over forty years of personal lived experience of compulsion and obsession, starting at the age of seven with a preoccupation with things needing to feel balanced. Over time, this evolved into tasks needing to be done to an excessive and unsustainably high standard.

I've seen five different psychotherapists over the years, each of whom has leaned into various theories. I found therapy both helpful and unhelpful. Different approaches provided unique benefits, but no single model or technique has ever proven to be a silver bullet. Psychological treatment for OCD, perfectionism and demanding internal standards can also be quite tricky for both the client and the therapist. Yet, the variety of approaches helped me bring different pieces together, eventually shifting my perspective, which then allowed me to shift gears.

Technically speaking, I no longer meet the clinical criteria for an obsessive-compulsive *disorder*. But I am still very much a compulsive and obsessive person. It is simply the case that it no longer dictates my life or generates the same degree of anxiety it once did. Yet, the tendency to check things and the demanding standards still hum in the background. When I say hum, they can fire up like the engines of a Boeing 747 taxiing for take-off, given the right conditions.

If you're wondering whether the rest of the book will be some life coaching-type pitch: "How I set myself free from OCD." It's not, and I did not. What I have learned to do is to recommission the small bombs of anxiety that trigger it and, over the years, have learned to drain the power from it. And no, it's not as simple as it sounds.

Of course, my experiences are not universal. OCD manifests in varied ways, and each person's journey is different. In my clinical work, I'm careful to bracket off my experiences so that I don't filter treatment through my personal lens. Although lived experience can be helpful to some degree in therapy, there is also a risk that it can skew the focus away from the person's individual experiences or lead to assumptions based on subjective leaps.

During the first chapter, I provide a basic outline of the current clinical understanding of OCD and obsessive-compulsive personality traits and how the lines between what is classed as a problem can often be quite blurred. However, the book is not about mental disease and illness; it's about real people, real lives, and what it is actually like to lose yourself and live life constantly on repeat.

The aim is to provide an honest reflection from a perspective that seeks to bridge the gap between clinical treatment and lived reality from both sides of the clinic room. The stories about my personal life and therapy experiences are all true. My family members have kindly provided their perspectives with consent to share these. However, any descriptions or references to patients in my clinical practice have been entirely fictionalised to ensure confidentiality. The therapists I've worked with have also been anonymised to protect their identities.

My own story is the primary case study that runs throughout, and I take a light-hearted view, which sometimes gets a little dark. Having worked with a lot of people with OCD over the years, I fully recognise that it is typically anything but light. However, I wanted to approach this book with honesty and integrity; it also has a bit of swearing in it—it's about real life. Hopefully, it will feel relatable in some ways and help to normalise similar or shared experiences.

At the very least, you will have an opportunity to analyse the shrink for once.

I hope you enjoy it.

1

Checking Boxes

Don't think of a polar bear, and you will see that the cursed thing will come to mind every minute
—Fyodor Dostoevsky

W ho is a compulsive and obsessive person?

Everyone experiences doubt, intrusive thoughts, and repeated patterns of behaviour. Literally all of us, this is human life. Checking that the gas hob is switched off before heading to bed isn't pathological; in most cases, it's sensible. The WhatsApp message you wrote, where you complain about your boss. Double-checking that you're sending it to your friend, not your boss, that's common sense. The difference between what is typical for someone versus a clinical problem is how much something causes difficulty, distress, or significantly interrupts how you want to live.

Are you doing things to an extreme? Does it negatively impact your personal sense of well-being, causing issues in your relationships? Are you constantly getting in your own way?

Imagine, while the rest of the world has checked the front door once and now getting on with their life, you've already checked it thirty-four times, to be precise. You're sweating, fluctuating between tears and fear because you "can't be late". Still, you circle back home again to "just make sure" the door didn't magically unlock itself. Then, you're angry with yourself because you know what you're doing is completely irrational, but you can't stop doing it. Now, having spent twenty minutes pulling the door off its hinges—you're late. For anyone who hasn't experienced OCD, of course, this sounds utterly bonkers unless you've lived it.

But it can be nearly impossible to describe to someone how hard it is to just "stop it".

This was me.

With obsessive-compulsive disorder (OCD), obsessions are the excessive attention that we pay to our own thoughts. They are typically intrusive, distressing, and unwanted. This is not to be confused with being infatuated and consumed with desire, as it is often portrayed in fiction novels and films. Nor am I talking about how someone can become dangerously fixated on another person, such as stalking.

Compulsions are the actions we take in response to disturbing thoughts, typically to manage the feelings and emotions generated by them or how we perceive and apply meaning to a particular context or situation. But it's important to understand that OCD isn't simply about illogical thoughts and peculiar habits. It can be pretty horrific and can cause a lot of problems.

Obsessions can centre on almost anything. For some, it's the fear of causing harm, such as accidentally starting a fire, missing a physical health symptom that leads to someone's death, or losing control and stabbing someone with a kitchen knife. Driving can become a minefield. I've worked with people who compulsively retrace their route via dashcam footage each day, convinced they've run someone over.

Others are tormented by thoughts of a sexual nature. These are typically shame-inducing and often overwhelming. Common themes include being plagued by distressing thoughts that they might have molested a child without realising it, or thoughts involving rape, abuse, or incest. The common denominator is the anxiety generated by them.

Then, there are those whose intrusive thoughts revolve around religion or morality. Scrupulosity can present as obsessive guilt about offending God, violating spiritual laws, or committing some form of moral blasphemy. The content often exceeds the person's cultural or religious baseline, which can make these types of intrusions all the more confusing and difficult to discuss.

Contamination fears can be common. These usually involve thoughts about the transfer of germs, bodily fluids, or unpleasant substances to the person through contact with their environment. The anxiety can be around being personally contaminated or being responsible for infecting others. Compulsions may include excessive handwashing and avoidance of touching contact points such as door handles. Some people avoid sex or perform cleansing rituals in secret.

However, not everyone can always identify a clear theme or thought that precedes their compulsive behaviours. That doesn't mean there isn't one. Our brains think constantly. But in some cases, the urge seems to arise from nowhere. People describe a need to touch, tap, adjust or blink because something doesn't feel "right" or "even". Clinically, this is common in symmetry or precision-based OCD. It's especially likely in people with a history of childhood tics.[1]

One of the more contested concepts in OCD is the notion of having only obsessions without any compulsions. The urban term *pure-O* emerged to describe this, referring to people who experience disturbing thoughts without any outward compulsive actions. However, the label is often seen as misleading. In most cases there are usually cognitive compulsions, including rumination, checking, repeating phrases, and mentally undoing or rehearsing scenarios. They function in the same way as physical compulsions, just carried out in the person's mind.[2][3]

Because both the obsession and the compulsion are cognitive, they can be harder to interrupt. You can redirect someone's attention, but you can't stop them from thinking altogether. Therapy focuses instead on helping people recognise when they're engaging in mental rituals and learning to respond differently to those urges.

For the vast majority of people, regardless of how disturbing the content of their thought is, the anxiety generated is the brain's misfiring alarm system. Irrespective of how intelligent or logical someone is, they can struggle to discriminate between fake news and real threat.

Similar to a smoke alarm, the life-preserving system of the brain will trigger if the house is on fire and everyone needs to escape, which is its primary purpose and function. Yet, for people with anxiety-based problems it will also activate when it senses the fumes from scorched toast, requiring a window opening rather than emergency services attending the scene.

OCD typically involves all smoke and no fire, but we still evacuate the building—just in case.

Most people with the features we more classically consider as OCD typically experience both their thoughts and actions as distressing or bothersome. They are very aware of the anxiety it generates and continue with compulsive actions despite them being irrational. That is, until you are no longer anxious and the healthier parts of the mind are back in the driving seat—until next time. Hence, many people need some help with managing the whole thing.

But imagine what it would be like to walk into a doctor's office, speak to a teacher after school, or a friend or family member. Explaining to them that you're having dark thoughts about sexually assaulting or stabbing children, that you may have grabbed your manager's genitals during a meeting of twenty people at work, or that you have the urge to plough your car into pedestrians at a zebra crossing.

That isn't easy to do.

With obsessive-compulsive personality, things are a bit different.

The concept has its roots in Freud's early psychoanalytic idea of the *anal character*, referring to people who were excessively ordered, rigid, and frugal. If you've ever been described as "anally retentive," this is where the term originated. Freud believed that these traits stemmed from unresolved psychological conflicts during the *anal stage* of psychosexual development, between the ages of twelve months to three years old.[4]

Naturally, this stage involves toilet training, where children develop a greater awareness of retention and expulsion, including external expectations around control and cleanliness. Granted, many adults have a tendency to hang onto metaphorical shit they'd be better getting rid of, but this doesn't necessarily mean that we have all been traumatised at the age of two years old. Most of us probably wouldn't even remember it if we had.

While Freud came up with some groundbreaking stuff, arguably still influential in modern practice, contemporary psychology draws from a range of models. These include varied personality trait theories and schema-based approaches to explain the development and maintenance of rigid, highly controlled personality styles.

Obsessive-compulsive personality disorder, or *OCPD,* isn't so much about rituals or explicit fears. It's about personality organisation rather than a list of symptoms.

Clinically, there are eight recognisable features according to the Diagnostic and Statistical Manual (DSM-5).[5] To meet the threshold, at least four of the criteria need to be consistently present from early adulthood.

First, there's a preoccupation with rules, order, lists, and schedules, often to the point that the primary task gets lost.

Then, there's perfectionism that interferes with output and productivity. Not just high standards but standards that are so rigid that nothing ever feels good enough or complete. Reports redrafted a dozen times. Essays that cannot be submitted unless they're likely to win a Nobel prize. Perceived failure if the essay is returned with an admirable mark but falls one point short of the last benchmark. Even minor errors can feel intolerable.

Workaholism and excessive hours of productivity tend to take priority over almost everything else. Time off doesn't feel earned, deserved, or warranted. Rest is rationed, if it's permitted at all. Friendships and hobbies become peripheral. This can also be projected outward, applied to coworkers or employees.

Moral thinking can also be quite black and white. Right is right, wrong is wrong, and there's often little room for ambiguity. Again, the same standards applied internally can also be applied to others, whether consciously done or not.

Delegating tasks can also be very difficult. Not because others are objectively incapable but because, subjectively, they're unlikely to do it in the exact way the person expects. Precision and attention to detail matters. The sheer frustration of watching someone do it differently often outweighs the benefit of letting them get on with it in their own way.

People can struggle with discarding things, even when those things have no sentimental or practical value. Broken electronics, decades-old paperwork, or packaging. This is not necessarily *hoarding* in a clinical sense; it's more resource-based, a refusal to waste things or to avoid future regret.

Money can follow a similar pattern. Spending can be significantly restrained, not because of actual financial hardship, but because of a compulsive need to save and stockpile. The idea of wasting cash is almost as uncomfortable as wasting time. Sometimes, people live life as though they are on the breadline despite having a million pounds in the bank. Obviously, this is quite an extreme example, labouring the point.

Many people have no option but to watch their spending. Others save for specific reasons, such as university fees for the kids, and retirement plans. Yet, if you're bathing in three inches of water, sitting shivering with the heating off in winter, but have a stack of cash gathering dust under the floorboards, then it's possible you may be a little closer to the obsessive-compulsive spectrum than just being "careful with money".

Finally, there's the broader sense of rigidity and stubbornness that extends into pretty much all aspects of functioning.

Changing plans, compromising on approach and feeling out of control tend to provoke a disproportionate level of distress.

Again, it's important to remember that what constitutes personality traits versus a *disorder* is the degree of negative impact associated with them. Many of you reading this will likely see yourself in some of the traits described. I still tick four of these boxes, but it's very unlikely that I would meet the clinical threshold for a formal diagnosis these days.

In various aspects of life, including the therapy room, I've met countless people who enjoy having things neat and tidy. My mother-in-law washes the inside of her bin, puts rubbish bags within bags and cleans everything she puts in them. Many people like a spotlessly clean house or live their lives in disciplined ways; they are always on time, hit deadlines early, and go the extra mile at work. This is not a clinical issue in the majority of cases.

Yet, you may be someone who is on your third marriage because no one can sustain your showroom standards in the house. Coworkers possibly feel redundant because you refuse to delegate tasks. A close friend or family member dies, and you first think, "I'm not sure I can take the time out for the funeral." Then, that might need a closer look.

For people with obsessive-compulsive personality traits, compulsions often present more subtly, in many cases outside of conscious awareness. Compulsive behaviours are generally more about maintaining control over an outcome and meeting internalised expectations. The actions are more typically rule-bound and MUST be done, not necessarily to manage immediate feelings.

In therapy-speak, the difference between OCD and obsessive-compulsive personality traits is commonly discussed in terms of *ego-dystonic* and *ego-syntonic* processes. This is simply a fancy way of saying that our thoughts are either contrary or out of sync with our more static traits and values (dystonic), or very much in keeping and aligned with them (syntonic).

Commonly, with OCD, the thoughts and images we experience are not aligned with our sense of self, such as intrusive thoughts about harming someone. Perfectionistic and demanding internal standards often match so well that it's difficult for people to recognise their destructive potential, often perceiving them as having benefit and value.[6]

My own patients will often arrive in therapy experiencing problems with anxiety and depression. Still, they usually won't recognise this to be the case. The catalyst for the onset of the issues will often relate to external factors: relationship problems, workplace stress, and loss, rather than excessive worry or concern about intrusive thoughts and images. Yet, when exploring the internally demanding standards, there is often pushback and resistance. I've been there myself.

Many fear that by taking their foot off the gas, even a tiny amount will somehow turn their life upside down, causing them to lose everything or be forced to accept *average* standards.[7] At least, from their viewpoint.

In clinical practice, I commonly see people with overlapping characteristics of both OCD and obsessive-compulsive personality traits. From my perspective, this makes recovery, particularly from OCD, much more challenging. Whether someone is repeatedly worrying that they are a paedophile, avoiding being near children due to distressing sexually intrusive thoughts, or they're trimming the front lawn with nail scissors at 2 am to prevent perceived criticism from the neighbours, they all involve internal processes that can be very difficult to counter.

While it is necessary to understand the fundamental differences between obsessive-compulsive problems, the evidence base behind the concepts and treatment approaches is somewhat shaky. Aside from the conflicting approaches from different schools of thought, the wealth of outcomes from randomised controlled research trials, while encouraging, rarely transfer to the reality of clinical practice.

As a clinician, I've commonly encountered large organisations wafting *evidence-based* speak at me. Which is important, and I get why. Research shows us what works.

Yet, both patients and practitioners are often sold popular methods of treatment, commonly cognitive and behavioural approaches. They can work, just not for everyone. For some people, particularly those with milder symptoms of OCD or more recent onset, approaches such as exposure and response prevention (ERP) can bring relief. It can be effective longer-term with the right balance of pace, intensity, and ongoing application around flare-ups.[8]

But these aren't the clients who typically walk through my door—nor was that the case for me in the early stages of my own therapy, often labelled "treatment resistant".

In clinical trials, outcomes are mixed. Around a third of participants show significant symptom reduction, and another third achieve full remission. But relapse is common.

Within a year of treatment, about half will experience a recurrence of symptoms.[9] There are many likely contributors to this: co-occurring mental health conditions, social stressors, and physical health issues. Teenagers tend to fare a little better, with around two-thirds experiencing significant improvement and nearly a third fully recovering.[10] That said, the rates of suicidal ideation are disproportionately higher in younger people, with around half reporting suicidal thoughts and nearly a quarter engaging in self-harm.[11]

Medication can help, but not without limits. Selective serotonin reuptake inhibitors (SSRIs), and sometimes SNRIs, are commonly prescribed to treat OCD. Like with many anxiety and mood-related conditions, these medications can reduce symptoms by dampening the nervous system's physiological response. This can make obsessions and compulsions feel more manageable. But they don't stop intrusive thoughts or directly alter the compulsions.

For people with perfectionistic personality traits, medication may be more effective in easing generalised anxiety or low mood related to chronic internal pressure. Arguably, SSRIs don't change personality.

It doesn't surprise me that the relapse rates following medication discontinuation are often much higher.[12] Combining ERP with medication may improve outcomes slightly, but the long-term benefit often hinges on continued support. Side effects are also common. Most people I've worked with report some degree of emotional numbing of positive emotions as a trade-off for reduced negative feelings.

Sexual side effects are also frequently reported. They don't discriminate by gender, including lowered sex drive, vaginal dryness, problems with erections, orgasm and ejaculation—brilliant! Needless to say, many of the patients I've worked with choose to switch or stop taking medication for these reasons. However, it's very important that people discuss any issues or unwanted side effects of taking medication with their prescriber before doing so.

While I may sound like a massive mood hoover here, I'm not anti-medication, nor am I averse to using CBT. Most of the guidance, particularly from the NHS, is that combining these treatments is typically the most effective for OCD. If you can tolerate them and you find it helps—great! If not, hopefully, the rest of the book will give you some hope that this is not the end of the road.

* * *

So, what is realistic?

Psychologists and psychotherapists can have a tendency to tinker with psychological models, and not necessarily always in a way that is backed up by research. We can often start putting our own stamp on things. At times, this is necessary, tailoring standardised treatment to individual needs. Other times, more our own personal worldview.[13]

As someone with rigid internal rules around doing things "correctly" for most of my life, and despite manualised therapy being my least preferred method of working, I've generally been a stickler for it, mostly due to the research base. Yet, I've rarely seen the outcomes produced by the randomised controlled trials mapping onto the nuance of clinical practice.

Many people require ongoing work, either through periodic episodes of therapy or broader support addressing emotional and cognitive patterns.

Often, I am the third, fourth, or fifth therapist someone has seen, which comes with pros and cons. On the one hand, there can be a lot of pressure to be a magician, the therapist who can unearth what others have failed to find before. Obviously, this is unrealistic; there are no perfect therapists, and the models of therapy I lean into are generally no different from those used by previous therapists.

The main advantage is the opportunity to explore what has already been tried. Less is the case that I am a brilliant or magical therapist. More the case that I have hindsight based on the prior legwork from the client and the therapists before me. And, from my own personal therapy experiences, I have the confidence to ask realistic, often very frank, direct questions from the outset.

A frequent barrier to treatment is misdiagnosis, the most common being generalised anxiety (GAD), especially when the symptoms are less overt or involve taboo content. Studies show that about half of OCD cases are misdiagnosed, with errors more likely when symptoms centre on sexual or violent thoughts.[14]

Over the last few years there has also been a significant increase in public awareness of mental health and other conditions—which is a good thing. I've been increasingly asked whether certain obsessive and compulsive symptoms might be better explained by autism or ADHD. The question tends to come up a lot in psychological assessments. And it's not an unreasonable question. On the surface, the behavioural aspects of both OCD and OCPD can look similar: repetitive actions, intolerance of uncertainty, difficulties with attention or flexibility.[15] But the reasons behind what is driving them are often quite different.

From my own lived experience of obsession and compulsion, neither my early developmental history, thinking patterns, nor how I experience the external world would indicate either autism or ADHD. However, for many people, they can coexist.[16] There is often a lot of overlap, and they can look very similar, even to a trained eye. But there are important differences.

OCD is classified as a mental health condition. It tends to develop during adolescence or early adulthood, although symptoms can appear earlier. Autism and ADHD are neurodevelopmental conditions. That means they're present from early life, even if they're not recognised at the time, and they affect how the brain processes information across a wide range of domains, not just in response to anxiety-inducing thoughts or rule-bound behaviour.[17]

Autism typically involves a range of differences in social communication, sensory processing, and cognitive flexibility. Many autistic people experience what's often called *masking* (copying others to blend in socially), which can be absolutely exhausting. There's often a strong need for routine, intense interests, and a struggle with unstructured or unpredictable situations. Repetitive behaviours, often termed *stimming*, typically serve a self-regulatory purpose, helping to calm or manage sensory overload.[18]

However, where this may relate to symmetry-based compulsions, there can be considerable overlap.

Regarding ADHD, the features tend to be more about attention regulation and impulse control. Traits typically show up by the age of twelve, often earlier, and they're experienced across multiple settings. For example, home, school, and social situations. People with ADHD may struggle with focus, organisation, memory, and time management. Hyperactivity might look like constant movement, excessive talking, or mental gymnastics, like being powered by batteries that don't switch off until they're entirely drained.[19] Parents often describe their children as "on the go all the time," with problems retaining information and difficulty following instructions.

Living with chronic disorganisation or underperformance due to problems with executive function, especially in structured environments like school, can wear away at self-esteem. It's not uncommon to see low mood or worry as secondary issues.[20]

All of this makes diagnosis more complicated than it looks on paper. I've had patients who technically met the criteria for all three: OCD, autism, and ADHD. Each of them had nuanced and individual experiences. The implications matter, though, at least in terms of how best to help the person.

Obsessive and compulsive problems are usually treated with psychotherapy and sometimes medication. Autistic people may need environmental adjustments, family education, and advocacy around school or employment.[21]

For people living with ADHD, this might involve practical structure, school adaptations, and, in some cases, prescribed stimulant medication, which can involve long-term physical health monitoring.[22]

All human traits exist on a spectrum, and people are more complex than checkboxes in a manual. Still, understanding which ballpark you are working with can significantly increase the likelihood of the person getting what they need.

So, how do you become a compulsive-obsessive person?

That would really depend on who you ask.

There are many theories, from faulty thinking, overexcited brain regions, and entrenched belief systems to emotional regulation and psychological conflicts.

From a cognitive-behavioural perspective, the cycle begins when we attach exaggerated meaning to our thoughts. We try to neutralise or keep them at bay through repeated actions.

Schema models take a broader developmental view. This is the idea that our early experiences shape deep-seated rules and beliefs about how the world works. If you grew up in chaos, you might learn that being highly controlled with clear rules brings more emotional safety. If love was conditional, being "perfect" might reduce the potential of rejection.

Neuroscience tends to lean into brain function. OCD has been linked to hyperactivity in certain regions involved in error detection, decision-making, and habit formation.[23] Neurotransmitters like serotonin and glutamate appear to play a role, as do certain genetic factors.[24] The brain registers threat, and the alarm senses scorched toast. Over time, this forms a *feedback loop*.

More traditional therapists, using psychodynamic theory, sometimes come from a different angle. Compulsions are seen as symbolic "defences" or strategies we unconsciously develop to manage impulses, feelings, or emotional discomfort that we can't fully process. It's less about the thought itself and more about what it represents. In this frame, the rigidity and control of OCPD might be ways to defend against vulnerability or emotional intimacy, especially if this felt dangerous or unpredictable in early life.

Each model brings something to the table, and from both my personal and clinical experience, there's a degree of truth to each of them. Yet, none of them explains everything. And if you live with OCD or perfectionistic traits, chances are you'll recognise bits of yourself in all of them.

Of course, as humans, we are a meaning-making species. We like to understand things and have clear answers. But when it comes to why we do what we do, there is rarely anything neat and tidy about it.

To understand this in the context of real human life, we need to go back to the very beginning.

2

Touching Stones

*The initial relationship between self and others
serves as a blueprint for all future relationships*
— John Bowlby

T ell me about your childhood.

Words that typically send my own patients into a spiral during their first appointment. Undoubtedly, the field of psychology and psychiatry often has a caricatured image of attributing our adult life problems to our parents or early guardians. However, personality formation and our perception of the social world are complex. There are key development stages from birth to adulthood that significantly shape our worldview. Hence, it's crucial to consider our historical timeline when we explore current psychological issues.

But we need to tread carefully There is no general benchmark or specific ideal that we are aiming to achieve with our clients. Recollection of early life is often sketchy to some degree. Human memory isn't entirely reliable, and we will each hold our own perspectives and interpretations of the same events.

What we can recall and how we recall it are shaped by many variables. Even memory that feels crystal clear or *photographic* may still be incomplete or subject to distortion.

Essentially, the human brain does not record and save information like a smartphone camera does; it reconstructs information, reassembles impressions and fragments, and pieces them together. Our current mood and emotional state can also affect how memories are recalled.[1] Clinical depression is associated with memory recollection that holds a negative bias and a tendency to interpret ambiguous events with pessimism.[2] Repetition, or constantly going over events, can also lead to memory becoming more intense and emotionally charged, regardless of the original intensity when it was first recalled.[3]

Even our recollection of significant events can become distorted. A well-known example comes from the psychologist William Hirst, who conducted a long-term study on *flashbulb memories*.[4] This is a term he uses to describe vivid, emotionally charged recollections formed during traumatic experiences.

Many people remember watching the first plane, American Airlines Flight 11, crash into the North Tower of the World Trade Centre live on television at 8:46 am on the morning of September 11, 2001. But that footage was never aired live. There were no news cameras filming the towers at that time. It was the second plane, United Airlines Flight 175, striking the South Tower 17 minutes later, that was filmed live on air.

Footage of the first crash was captured by Jules Naudet, a documentary filmmaker who happened to be filming firefighters in Manhattan that morning. His footage wasn't released by the media until several hours later.

Now, imagine if footage of the first plane had never surfaced. Our memory of that first impact would be shaped entirely by secondary information: images of the burning tower and news commentary recorded after the fact. So, we might turn to eyewitness accounts to fill in the gaps. Some of the eyewitnesses described seeing a small aircraft flying toward the towers. Yet, Flight 11 was a large commercial airliner. Eventually, we'd be left to piece together what happened using flight path data, specialist engineers, and forensic analysis of the site.

Essentially, human memory is subjective and not always made up of the full facts. Many of us also struggle to recall memories from our very early lives in great detail.

As psychologists and therapists, we're generally pretty good at objectively finding problems you didn't know were problems until you walked into the room. Obviously, any decent therapist isn't trying to help you invent your history or dictate it to you. Nevertheless, most people are somewhat apprehensive about exploring their early relationships, especially where this may involve confronting sensitive topics that they have limited recollection of and may not fit, despite sounding plausible.

I've been there. It's not an easy process, regardless of which chair you are sitting in. What I can safely say is that if you consider your early life to have been "completely perfect," void of any mistakes or flaws; maybe striving to be a perfect parent yourself—you may want to sit down.

I have bad news.

Perfect parents don't exist.

Like all humans, everyone has flaws, and we all make mistakes. Children can drive their parents crazy at times, scream all night, and fight with their siblings. Naturally, parents can both love and hate their children simultaneously. It's part of everyday life.

Working as a therapist, I've learned firsthand that regardless of how much showboating parents may do at the school gates, no matter how much they manufacture an *Instagram* life, rarely are things so gold-plated behind the scenes. For most of us, we do our best. Our parents or guardians raised us with what they had available to them at the time. And if we are very honest with ourselves, most of us would likely do things differently in our daily lives, with foresight. For that, we would need a crystal ball.

Sadly, some children experience terror at the hands of their caregivers. Some are severely neglected by them or are not kept safe by them. This is not uncommon to hear as a trauma therapist. In cases involving significant abuse, violence, or life-threatening situations, these are the types of events that the brain can sometimes struggle to process and can lead to complex emotional problems, difficulty creating and maintaining relationships, and mental health problems.

Of course, some people with OCD will have experienced these kinds of events or struggle with additional concerns, such as post-traumatic stress (PTSD). In my experience working across primary, secondary and specialist NHS services, as well as the private sector, it's more common to find that obsessive-compulsive tendencies, including perfectionism, are typically fuelled by clusters of memories commonly referred to as "small-t" traumas, feeding the narrative in the background.

Small-t traumas are adverse life events that vary in quality, severity, and impact. They can be single experiences we've witnessed or difficulties we've personally experienced: emotional neglect, bullying, humiliation, illness, or loss. These events can occur during our formative years when we establish our primary attachments or later in life, such as during school or early adulthood. They may not be as explicit as significant abuse or violence. However, they can still influence our emotional well-being and relationships for some time to come.

So, am I implying here that obsessive-compulsive problems are a trauma response?

No. At least this isn't the case for everyone.

It doesn't necessarily mean that negative or bad experiences directly lead to mental health issues. We all experience life in our own ways, and our brains will appraise information differently from our unique reference points. Still, these can stem from even the most ordinary life experiences.

———————— ✦ ✳ ✦ ————————

Meet Toby, an excitable four-year-old who loves the freedom he feels when he skips up and down the aisles of the local supermarket. Of course, he's excited, supermarket skating was ace! No longer a thing due to health and safety, but this is the Autumn of 1993.

It's a busy Saturday afternoon, and Toby's mother is trying to weave the shopping trolley around the crowds. She briefly stops to tend to her newborn, who has just vomited in the carrier strapped to the trolley. She's distracted and, for a brief moment, loses sight of her four-year-old.

Toby is oblivious. He is more focused on where he can see a gap in the crowd—a chance to run and slide on the smooth, polished supermarket floor. Then, a Teenage Mutant Ninja Turtle action figure grabs his attention in the toy section. He wrote to Santa asking for one last week, and he can't resist picking it up.

Turning to check where his mother is, he spots a woman with long brown hair and a beige coat pushing a trolley. He sets off in the same direction, trying to stay close to her.

Toby reaches out to hold her hand. He's been thinking about his letter to Santa. "Have I been a good boy this year, Mummy?" Now, looking up to see an unfamiliar face. Toby is scared and lost.

His mother has been frantically manoeuvring the trolley and the baby up and down the aisles. She's been calling out, but her voice is drowned by the Whitney Houston cover versions playing over the speakers.

Suddenly, the music stops, and there's a high-pitched screech of microphone feedback.

"If you are the mother of a small child called Toby, wearing a blue coat, please go to the customer service desk and ask to speak to Delia."

Immediately releasing the breath she has been holding, she starts shaking with relief. Toby is standing smiling at the store manager, but is now struggling to stop his mouth from doing a U-turn at the sight of his mother. He starts sobbing and runs over to cuddle her. She soothes him, thanks the supermarket staff and pays for her groceries.

As soon as they leave the store, Toby's mother bends down, firmly holding his arm. Now, with venom in her throat and a face so sharp that it could strip Artex from the ceiling.

"Don't you EVER run away from me like that again!"

Toby's face turns crimson, his eyes close, his mouth opens wide, and a momentary silence hangs in the air like lead.

The eye of the storm.

Then, the high-pitched wailing of a dysregulated four-year-old sweeps the supermarket car park. Toby continues to scream, becoming so distressed that he loses his breath—coughing.

His mother is now clinging to the baby carrier strapped to the shopping trolley; her newborn is vomiting for a second time. Her other hand grabbing hold of the hood of Toby's coat—which is the only available option she has to stop him running away.

Eventually, she reaches the car, steadying the trolley with her foot, opens her handbag using her teeth, grabs the last of the wet wipes, and cleans the vomit from her baby. She then picks Toby up to secure him in his car seat. As she lifts him, Toby intentionally whacks his baby brother.

Now, with two youngsters in a highly emotional state, she holds Toby's hands together while clicking his car seat into place and speaks to him calmly but firmly. "When we get home, you are going straight to bed. No cartoons! And, if you EVER hit your little brother again, I'm writing to Santa Claus to tell him to cancel your Ninja Turtle."

Toby goes quiet and looks down at his shoes.

Exhausted and on the edge of tears, she finally closes the door and puts the key in the ignition.

Toby starts screaming again.

"I HATE YOU—I WANT DADDY!"

Attempting to swallow the painful feelings in her stomach rising like acid, she hasn't the energy left to cope—she gives in.

"FINE! GO LIVE WITH DADDY!
I'VE HAD ENOUGH OF YOU!"

Toby starts screaming again—coughing, then vomits down the front of his coat. His mother has no energy left. No wet wipes to clean him up. She turns the key, starts the engine and drives the short distance home with the window wound down.

Nightmare! But it happens.

Kids get lost in supermarkets all the time. Stressed parents lose their cool with their kids on a daily basis. As adults, our brains can forecast the real and possible danger and harm that could come to a lost child in a supermarket. Even more so when they're trying to run across a busy car park.

Obviously, shouting, threats and punishment are not ideal ways to deal with a four-year-old having a meltdown. Yet, it's easier said than done when you're in the middle of it. It also doesn't mean that Toby's mother is a terrible parent for threatening to cancel Christmas. Families in many countries across the globe have been using threats of a fictitious, omnipresent bloke with a beard to get their children to behave for at least one hundred years, since around 1864 in England.

From a detached adult perspective, we can feel compassion for Toby. A young kid dealing with parental separation, his new baby brother is taking his mother's attention. We can also offer compassion and understanding toward Toby's mother. The context she was faced with was something most of us would find challenging. I certainly would.

But let's say Toby experiences mental health problems in later life and seeks out a psychological therapist. There are many ways this could go. During his first few sessions, he would likely develop a formulation or case conceptualisation with the therapist. This is a core part of most therapeutic models. In simple terms, a formulation is a working theory about what's going on right now and how both the client and therapist will go about helping the person to tackle it.

Different types of therapists do it in various ways. The range of theories we draw from is vast. Therapists typically lean into the models they are trained in and mostly draw from principles that make the most sense to them. Naturally, the same person could see five different therapists, and you would see five variations of how the problem developed.

This doesn't necessarily mean one is right and the others are wrong. While the models of therapy differ, we are often all talking about similar things, just using different terms and language to explain them. But psychotherapy, more broadly, is not a neutral process. Most therapists will have a theoretical lens that guides them to different areas of focus in their approach.

Perhaps Toby has developed a belief that he must always be "good" to avoid punishment. That he is not "enough" to prevent his father from walking out or comparing his worth, being left sitting in his own vomit, stinking, foul and acidic, compared to his shiny baby brother smelling like a fresh wet wipe.

Maybe he learns that from an early age, his mother cannot tolerate strong emotion, which leads to her withdrawing, equating anger and rage with emotional withdrawal and rejection. Might Toby be acting out these early dynamics in his adult relationships, leading to a chronic fear of emotional expression, always prioritising others, hiding perceived faults and flaws, with his foot on the emotional brakes?

Actually, all are perfectly plausible. Most of these examples could have been percolating in my head if Toby's mind had gone to this memory when describing his current difficulties. Yet, it would all remain in my head until more consistent patterns became clear and, importantly, discussed from the client's perspective in the here and now.

If you constantly attempt to avoid criticism, humiliation, or shame, and fear closeness in relationships, is it possible that somewhere along the way you learned to do this?

Of course! But how this came to be is often highly unique to the person.

It's also important to consider that there is a commercial side to the well-being industry; social media has given rise to many therapy-oriented platforms, often taking theoretical concepts and presenting them as universal truths. "You were taught you were too much to handle." "You were conditioned to self-abandon." But how does any of this actually directly relate to you if the person saying it has never sat in a room with you or given you space to talk about your life?

Granted, there is a lot of good information in the public domain, but there's also quite a bit of nonsense.

So, rather than me making massive assumptions and schooling you about what has *clearly* happened to *you* in *your* life, I'll let you analyse mine instead.

My own parents weren't perfect, but I was well looked after and kept safe, and like Toby, I got lost in the thrills of supermarket skating myself on several occasions.

My entrance into the world was quite a tad dramatic. I was a large baby against my mother's tiny frame, awkwardly positioned with the umbilical cord wrapped around my neck, refusing to move. An uncanny metaphor for what would later become my adult personality.

Needless to say, there were medical complications. My poor mother. Already a worrier, body wrecked by her first kid, and feeling helpless with uncertainty. Given this was the late 1970s in a small coal mining town in Yorkshire, the minute she could pee and stand without bleeding, they discharged her from the local maternity ward.

"Tha'l be reet, lass!"

Birth trauma wasn't recognised at the time, at least not to the degree it is today. The only psychologists waiting in the wings of the maternity wards were monitoring signs of severe mental distress and preparing for admission to the psychiatric unit.

I was a blue-grey colour and had to be placed under special lights for a while. Mum would sit frantically at the side of the incubator for hours. She was told by the doctors that due to hypoxia, there was a good chance that my brain had been damaged. I would require monitoring over the first year of my life to know for sure.

The first time I mentioned to my mum that I was writing this book, mostly trying to gauge how she felt about it, she told me a story about the first time she took me into our local town centre. I was just a few weeks old.

Mum left me in my pram outside the pharmacy. This seems alarming by today's standards, but this was in a time and place where this was a normal thing to do. She was also still recovering from giving birth, worrying about brain damage, all at the tender age of eighteen. She collected her prescription and carried on with her shopping. A while later, she was paying for groceries at the till when she suddenly felt the overwhelming sense that she had forgotten something—that would be me! Crying frantically, running across the town centre, she found me still parked outside the pharmacy, blissfully unaware, just watching the clouds go by from my pram.

Over the first few months of my life, the health visitors offered increasing reassurance that I was mostly showing signs of being a bright kid and was hitting my milestones. Over the next twelve months, Mum took it upon herself to repeatedly measure the circumference of my head, propping me up against the living room wall to observe my reflexes. She monitored every sound and movement, comparing this against the vast number of medical textbooks she had started stockpiling.

By the time of my terrible twos, I would sit quietly colouring things in, making shapes out of Play-Doh, or playing with the dog. But at night, I would relentlessly scream, demanding that my mother come into my room.

I would do the same if Dad tried to look after me while she was out. Obviously, there were signs of a funky attachment. Also, a lot to navigate as young parents.

My dad tended to encourage me to get involved in things, and like a lot of dads, he tried to get me interested in sports—I wasn't a fan. One evening, he spent the entire night cutting up an old sheepskin rug to make a wizard costume to enter me into a fancy dress competition at the pub over the road. I put it on in the house. I don't remember it, but I've seen a picture. It was pretty impressive, but I flatly refused to go and started screaming at any attempt at bribery.

When I started nursery, I still didn't like being separated from my mum, preferring her in my line of sight at all times. Despite attempts from the nursery staff to retain my attention, I would drag a chair across the room, grab my coat, and attempt to set off walking home. I was a determined and demanding child who could quickly see through pointless attempts at distraction and false rewards. In my mother's words, "You were a child who could not be bought."

Mum was on speed dial to Santa, the Tooth Fairy, the Easter Bunny—anyone that would pick up. I'd already caught on at a young age that these were urban myths.

"Go ahead—call them!"

Naturally, it was enough to put anyone off having more kids by this point. But Mum was pregnant with my sister, and I had mixed feelings about it. "If we don't like her when she arrives, can we send her back?" Essentially, any remaining nerves that were still intact when she brought me home from the hospital were well and truly frazzled by the time I was four.

Thankfully, I eventually settled. No longer demanding and screeching at night. But now fiercely independent and flatly refusing to do anything I did not wish to do—unless I saw sense in it. A trait that remains well-established, but arguably with more flexibility in my adult life.

Dad was hardworking and spent most of my early life doing overtime down the mine. His own parents died young, and he grew up experiencing poverty. Possibly what drove him to work relentless hours to ensure that his own family didn't go without. He went skydiving in his sixties and is now comfortably retired into his seventies; he's still constantly pursuing new projects to keep him occupied and travelling the globe in search of lesser known parts of the world As a young man, he had a short fuse at times, a family trait on both sides, but was the polar opposite of Mum in many ways.

I began straddling the line between typical and atypical behaviour around primary school age. Obviously, I didn't know it at the time. No one sat me down and told me what I was doing was compulsive.

It isn't easy to put things into words when you are seven. Very hard to explain why you have suddenly started getting the urge to touch the floor when walking over a crack in a paving slab.

Naturally, it started drawing attention from strangers. "Why is your kid always touching the floor?" The doctors told my mother that I would likely grow out of it. I did, but I started counting in my head instead. There was no particular reason other than odd numbers were bad—apart from the number seven. The number four was best—my favourite number.

I didn't have thoughts about my parents dying; there was no catastrophic event being averted. At least, neither my mother nor I remember this. It was just a feeling of things being off, perhaps mild dread.

Of course, these rituals can be common in children; some grow past them or can be easily guided away with parental encouragement. Unfortunately, in one way or another, mine stuck around for another thirty-five years.

Granted, you don't need to be Sigmund Freud to work out that my combined neuroticism and workaholism in adulthood likely have their roots in the modelling from my early family life: a classic anxious and preoccupied mother and an absent and distant father. That's the book done right there, then?

Well—not quite so fast.

Contrary to popular theories around perfectionism, neither of my parents was particularly pushy or overly critical. I was taught to be kind. Neither of them had any huge career expectations of me, apart from the fact that they wanted to make sure I could get a job and manage life as an adult. Like most parents, they just wanted me to be happy.

In my therapeutic work, I definitely see patterns of thought and action more typical of theory. These persist beneath the surface, manifesting in surges of anxiety, shame, or melancholy. But there are also many where this feels like a clunky fit.

Working in private practice, it's not uncommon for high-achieving professionals to sit in therapy, frustrated by their own success. Feeling trapped.

Often citing trending phrases.

"I think I have impostor syndrome!"

Perhaps?

A few sessions in, we uncover the voice of a long-forgotten teacher who told them, aged nine, that they would never amount to anything. "You better buck your ideas up!" Fast forward to the present day. That old message is just so familiar that it sounds like their own thoughts. Often flaring up around times of change, increased pressure or transition.

The bottom line being, that we have all faced adversity in childhood in one way or another. Most children adapt over time, developing resilience as their brains process the life experiences they encounter.

There's rarely a straight line between early life experiences and the intrusive thoughts or compulsions that emerge later. But more often than not, there's a touchstone—clusters of events and memories, usually fragmented or locked in the emotional perspective of a much younger self. Lost and naked from the broader helpful context that may make better sense of it in the here and now.

It's a lot to digest. I get it. For some, it will feel like a stretch, perhaps unnecessarily complicated theory. We can't change the past, so why focus on it? Is it simply better to cut to the chase and focus on response prevention and behavioural experiments? Trot off to the GP for 100mg of Sertraline?

Maybe? But if there are established unconscious blocks to implementing those things, how do we understand them if we are blind to them?

3

Adolescence

A stumble may prevent a fall
— Thomas Fuller

I t's easy to forget how difficult it was to be a teenager.

Navigating peer relationships, struggling to fit in, and rejection. Strange body changes, comparing ourselves to others, sexual maturation and experimentation. Some people look back on adolescence as being the best years of their lives. For me, it's all a bit of a mixed bag.

On the upside, the 1980s-1990s were the age of electronic synth. I can still feel the rush of electricity through my body from the opening bars of Björk's *Army Of Me* thundering around Sheffield Arena live in concert. On the downside, I hated school. Absolutely hated it. Anxiety also robbed me of a lot of my formative years.

I attended a regular comprehensive school, bright and academically capable, but I was bored to death and admittedly quite lazy. I wasn't a savant; my brain didn't simply want more complex work. Besides science and creative subjects such as music, I found the lessons dry and uninteresting, and my mind would wander. Constantly distracted by worry, I would often stare out of the window to switch off from my thoughts. Occasionally, I would be pulled up by the teachers. Most of them just left me to it.

Psychology wasn't on the curriculum, and I've played out the common question that therapists often ask.

"What piece of advice would you give your younger self?"

Honestly? If I could show my younger self live video footage of where I would be thirty years later, thirteen-year-old me wouldn't be interested. Having the foresight that I would eventually be working eighty-hour weeks and sitting endless exams would leave my ears ringing and blur my vision. Back then, I lived for the freedom of the weekend and school holidays, reading *Smash Hits,* riding my bike, playing with the dogs, and spending most Sunday evenings feeling sick during term time.

Like many teenagers, I experienced episodes of targeted bullying and conflict. This was partly because I was short and quiet and hung out with an eclectic group. The other part? Well, teenagers can be highly unpleasant to each other at times. It was part of growing up in this time and place. Needless to say, until starting psychodynamic therapy, it was a period in my life that I had locked firmly away in a lead-lined box. A different life.

Common with teenagers, I would hear lots of boys at school talking about porn. I was mostly clueless but pretended I knew what they were talking about. These were the days before the internet, so it wasn't readily available, and you had to be well-connected to get hold of it.

Some kids had an older brother, and they would rifle through their stash. The odd few had a dad with a secret drawer in the garden shed. One boy became an overnight rock star when his uncle, who worked at the newsagent's, gave him access to the "top shelf" in exchange for a month's pocket money. His uncle was later sent to prison for dealing weed from the back of an ice cream van, and the boy went back to being a face in the crowd.

Me? I was a misfit, not connected to the popular kids, with a nine-year-old sister who was into My Little Pony. We didn't have a garden shed. I didn't know anyone at the corner shop and was too short to reach the top shelf by myself.

But, like most thirteen-year-olds, I was allowed to be alone in the house for brief periods, and I would take the opportunity to indulge the developing parts of my psyche. By this age, I was becoming aware that I was a bit odd. Different interests from the other kids.

I was struggling but trying to keep it secret and hidden.

My parents set off with my sister one Saturday afternoon to the local supermarket. I heard the car start on the drive and ran to my sister's bedroom window, watching them pull away. This was my chance. Desperately waiting since last night.

There was a strong sense of guilt opening the door to my parents' bedroom. I knew I shouldn't be in there. As I opened my mum's wardrobe, an intense rush of adrenaline flooded me with anxiety. Slightly nauseous, carefully making a mental image. Everything would need to be put back exactly where it was—no one must notice I had been in there.

My friends wouldn't understand. My dad? Well, he really wouldn't get it. If my mother found out, I would probably get into trouble.

There it was, I could see it. Sandwiched between Dr Miriam Stoppard and The British National Formulary.

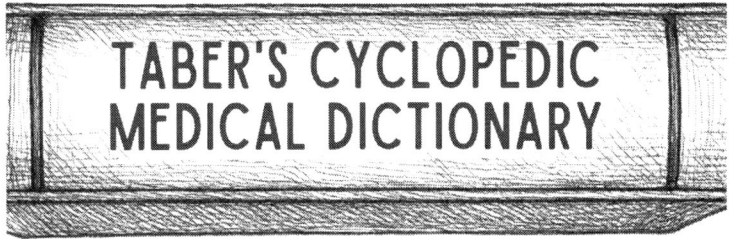

Taber, C. W. (1989). Cyclopedic Medical Dictionary (16th ed.)

On Friday nights, we were allowed to stay up late to watch TV. A news story about a global spike in deadly bacteria causing necrosis had aired on the BBC. Strains of group A Streptococcus were infecting open wounds. Despite the spike, it was still rare and sensationalised by the media, typically only affecting people during open heart surgery.

Regardless, I'd just had a benign lump cut off my ankle at the hospital. Minor procedure with a tiny bit of local anaesthetic. But I was suddenly convinced the scab was darkening and going black at the edges. I stayed up all night monitoring and scrutinising it. I didn't want to lose my leg to necrotising fasciitis, and I definitely didn't want to die from it.

There would be many times I would return to the wardrobe to diagnose my fantastical ailments. By the age of fifteen, I had survived flesh-eating bacteria, HIV-AIDS, Creutzfeldt-Jakob disease, pulmonary embolism, subarachnoid haemorrhage, three heart attacks and two brain tumours. All without a single day off sick from school—a miracle of modern science. Each ailment correlated with news stories or educational programs on the BBC.

Needless to say, I wasn't getting much of a mainstream education at the local comp, but I was giving Oxford Medical School a run for its money at home.

By the final years of high school, my compulsions had built up. Some made a degree of logical sense. We had a pet cockatiel called Woody that flew away because the door was accidentally left open. Luckily, we managed to get him back; he could mimic human language and pick up on the words spoken in the house. Whenever I entered the living room, he chirped, "LOCK THE DOOR!" But I'd already checked it several times.

I would press the fridge door repeatedly to ensure it was firmly shut. This was to prevent the family from being struck down by Vibrio vulnificus, a pathogenic bacterium commonly associated with marine life, including shellfish. There was a rise in people dying of it in Mexico. I'd heard it on the news.

It didn't necessarily affect the Marks & Spencer prawns my mum bought in Wakefield, but they were definitely shellfish. Who knew for certain where they were from?

Some compulsions made no sense at all. I would press the buttons on the portable TV in my bedroom (these were the days before remote controls). I would have to do this in a particular sequence, often repeating it until it felt right. This was to make sure that I didn't die in my sleep.

There were odd ones. Mentally separating good zones and bad zones in my bedroom. Good numbers and bad numbers. Missing every third step on the staircase to land on the fourth step. Our house had thirteen steps, so I would jump on the last one and say "four" in my head. Obviously, I was more at risk of causing my own death than preventing the death of others, but the risk of not doing it felt high.

At times, turning my head at a peculiar angle to look at the TV to neutralise thoughts about the house blowing up, despite my dad being a miner and everything in the house being either coal-powered or electric, not gas.

No one at home really noticed. They were subtle in front of other people, with the physical compulsions done out of sight or alone. Going on for hours if no one was home.

* ✳ *

So, why does a physically healthy teenager start preoccupying themselves with disease, illness and death?

There have been several terms to describe it over the years. Some have been established in language, certainly in Westernised communities. "They've always been a bit of a hypochondriac," often with a pejorative edge.

The term hypochondriasis dates back to ancient Greek medicine, originally used to describe discomfort or pathology believed to originate from the area beneath the rib cartilage, or *hypochondrium*. It was typically a diagnosis given when medicine had no other explanation.

Something was happening "under the cartilage" but remained invisible to the diagnostic tools of the time.[1] These days it has been largely replaced in clinical use by more specific diagnoses like illness anxiety disorder and somatic symptom disorder.[2] To meet diagnostic criteria, the health anxiety must persist for at least six months and not be better explained by another problem, such as OCD or generalised anxiety (GAD).

Commonly, people will frequently visit medical doctors, request investigations and scans, and seek constant reassurance. Sometimes, the complete opposite, avoiding medical settings altogether due to a fear of being told they may actually have something physically wrong with them. Again, as with any psychiatric diagnosis, it has to have a marked impact on daily life and occupational functioning.[3]

For me, this is where things start to get a bit messy. Mental health diagnosis relies on conceptual frameworks; there are checklists and guidelines, but it's rarely black and white. In my own experience, health anxiety has spanned features of both

OCD and generalised worry. Technically, I met the criteria for all three: OCD, GAD, and health anxiety.

That's also been the case for many of the patients I've worked with over the years. In the majority of those situations, the formal diagnosis they had been previously given was either GAD or depression. Often, they were seen by medics as an anxious person who's a bit of a nuisance, frequently turning up to GP appointments or A&E after late-night Googling, self-diagnosis, or panic symptoms.

And I can fully understand why that might be frustrating for a medical professional, particularly when your main tools are blood tests, scans, and antidepressants.

The problem is, while diagnostic labels rarely capture the full picture of someone's experience, they do shape the treatment approaches people are offered. First-line treatment for depression, for example, tends to lean towards *behavioural activation*, getting someone into a steady routine of sleep, exercise, essential tasks, and pleasurable activity.

Generalised anxiety tends to be approached with techniques like mindfulness, breathing exercises, worry diaries, and learning to tolerate uncertainty. But health anxiety often involves *safety behaviours*, such as checking and reassurance seeking, which start to resemble compulsions. It's also very common to see an increased sensitivity to internal cues, like physical sensations or bodily changes, such as heart palpitations or tension headaches.

The most widely accepted framework for understanding health anxiety is the cognitive and behavioural model by

Salkovskis and Warwick (2001).[4] It considers pre-existing beliefs about health and illness, often shaped by early experiences, and the interpretation of bodily sensations as dangerous. The behavioural components: constant checking, seeking reassurance, and avoiding triggers, are negatively reinforced, reducing anxiety in the short term but ultimately preventing disconfirmation of the fear over the long term.

Sound familiar?

Exposure and response prevention (ERP), adapted from its use in OCD, can be particularly effective. People are gradually exposed to health-related fears while refraining from checking or reassurance-seeking. Sometimes behavioural experiments are employed, exposing the person to the feared outcome at its fullest conclusion, as Gill did with me. For those with particular sensitivity to sensations and changes in the physical body, interoceptive exposure (exposure to internal experiences) can also be helpful.

Still, having spent years as a patient with health anxiety myself, I've often found it frustrating to be handed an information sheet declaring, "Your thoughts are not facts." Like many people with health anxiety, our heads are often full of facts. Medical ones. It's not just random nonsense pulled from the internet. After years of reading and researching disease and illness, our minds can start to resemble a medical Rolodex, packed with information on everything from common heart conditions and cancers to obscure diseases found in two people in the Himalayas.

The problem isn't a lack of facts; it's the lack of medical training needed to interpret how all of it fits together in realistic and practical terms. Many symptom clusters can point to both self-limiting, benign conditions as well as serious, life-threatening illnesses.

Essentially, the goal of psychological treatment is not to eliminate worry or thoughts or to perfect knowledge about health. Instead, it attempts to help someone increase their adaptive capacity to tolerate ambiguity. It does not try to stop them from seeking medical advice for health concerns, but it does help them bring this into balance, reduce the tendency to leap to conclusions and build trust in professional advice.

Another problem here is the million-dollar question.

"What is the priority for treatment?"

Is it obsession and compulsion, or worry that is driving the person to distraction, or depression stemming from the constant life restriction and persisting fear? This is often difficult for someone to pull all of this apart. It can take quite a bit of time to really understand the more lived experience of how this impacts someone's life. In some cases, it can also be tricky to navigate whose priority it is.

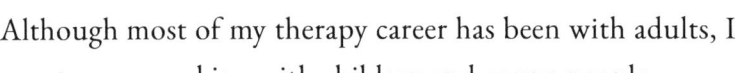

Although most of my therapy career has been with adults, I spent a year working with children and young people.

On one hand, it was a potent reminder that childhood and adolescence are critical developmental stages in human psychology. On the other hand, it was also a reminder of why being a teenager was something I would never want to repeat unless I could go back in time with the knowledge I have now.

Anxiety in children often presents through physical complaints, such as headaches, stomach aches, and fatigue. Usually, persisting despite normal medical results. Sometimes, this is referred to in clinical terms as *somatising*.[5] Unlike adults, children may not articulate explicit fears about illness and health. Still, their behaviour can indicate a preoccupation: attempts to avoid school, asking repeated questions about their health, or constantly checking their bodies. Sometimes, these are also subtle early markers for OCD.[6] Again, it is commonly misdiagnosed as generalised anxiety or sometimes interpreted as behavioural problems such as opposition or defiance.

The young people I worked with were mostly teenagers, aged thirteen to seventeen. Around a third of my caseload involved trauma cases (PTSD). The rest were struggling with anxiety, depression, and OCD. I was also navigating new clinical territory—the client's parents!

As you might have gathered by now, early caregivers often come up in therapy, whether the client is seven or seventy. But with adults, you rarely meet them. The boundaries of treatment are usually clearer too; what's said in therapy stays in therapy unless there's a serious risk of harm. With young people, this varies much more, depending on age, risk, and capacity to consent. Parental involvement tends to be higher with younger children, often focusing on helping the family work together. With teenagers and young adults, it varies as they develop autonomy.

As with adults, themes related to intrusive thoughts were often shaped by news stories or offhand comments from parents or peers. But OCD can shift quickly between themes, turning therapy into a kind of psychological Whack-a-Mole. It didn't take long before I started to empathise with the sheer exhaustion many parents described.

Still, understanding what maintains the problem can be complicated, especially when parents are understandably frustrated. The young person can sometimes be seen as the source of something that needs to be "fixed". At times, to ease the parents' anxiety.

Other times, because of challenges like school refusal or pressure from local authorities. In some families, this creates competing needs. Parents may feel worn down, dismissed, or overwhelmed. Meanwhile, the young person can feel misunderstood or scrutinised, and these dynamics can be difficult to navigate as a therapist.

Most of us have heard the term "helicopter parenting".[7] It's used to describe overly involved guardians. While it often comes from a place of care, I'm not really a fan of the term. I find it a bit unfair, at least in its general form.

The modern world poses significant risks, many of which are online these days, and our young people face a lot of vulnerability from the social world. A degree of covert hovering from a distance is possibly quite sensible.

But helicopters can be tricky, though.

It can also depend on which one.

Eye in the sky: Teens with parents who constantly monitor them may struggle to develop autonomy and decision-making skills, becoming overly reliant on external authority rather than learning to navigate grey areas. This can delay emotional maturity and reduce confidence in their own judgement. It may also hinder resilience when faced with real-world challenges.

News anchor: Teens whose parents overshare may struggle with self-consciousness and a disrupted sense of personal boundaries. Feeling exposed can make it harder to trust others. Privacy is crucial for identity development; without it, they may become guarded, anxious, or disconnected, fearing public humiliation and internalising shame.

Medivac: When parents are hyper-focused on health and safety, teens can absorb a sense that the world is dangerous or their bodies are fragile. This can fuel health anxiety or a heightened fear of discomfort or failure. It may also interfere with risk-taking, which is developmentally necessary for growth. Resilience requires some distress tolerance.

Apache: Overly dismissive, critical or aggressive parenting can leave teens constantly on edge, doubting their worth or bracing for attack and fear seeking help. They may internalise harsh criticism or develop perfectionism to avoid being *shot down*. This can create a fear-driven approach to life, where failure feels catastrophic. Resilience doesn't thrive under fire—it needs space to fail safely and recover.

Some parents are anxious, often self-blaming, and some are entirely hands-off. But when it comes to OCD, most feel a bit lost, unsure how to help. While biology and temperament may indeed contribute, the emotional environment and adult responses can be influential in the child's management of it. Particularly, the sense of support a young person experiences can affect their willingness to speak up.

———————— * ✳ * ————————

During my mid-teens, my mother and I were not aware that we had established a reciprocal maintaining pattern. We were both health anxious and feeding each other's anxieties. Yet, it wasn't quite as cut and dry as it appears in textbooks. Mum could be very sensible and pragmatic when it came to other people, particularly my health worries; given the amount of medical paraphernalia she had, it was like living with a GP.

She simply gave medical facts as to why my worry was unlikely, challenging the conclusions I would jump to. Sometimes, she could settle my mind quickly, but it would fire up again soon after.

Naturally, she would become exhausted with it all and get annoyed with me and the relentless new threads I would pull. I knew it bothered her, so I intentionally limited the reassurance seeking myself.

Instead, I would work things out independently, sourcing from her medical books without the required medical training to put them into context. However, Mum also struggled to contain her own anxieties when she was worried or ruminating about something, particularly when it came to her kids. A tendency to get an idea in her head that would rapidly escalate from adding two plus two and make a massive leap to twenty-five.

I was about fifteen at the time, sitting in a maths class, staring out the window, deep in thought—just not about maths. I began stirring a little in the present, a muffled voice calling my name. Then, in full stereo—"JAMES SPIERS!" Startled, I turned to look at the teacher who stood with the school secretary at the door. "Your mum is waiting in reception to take you to your emergency dental appointment."

My what?!

Walking to the reception area, I was worrying. My last check-up was only a few months ago. Had they found oral cancer and not told me about it?

My teeth felt fine.

As soon as I saw my mum, I knew her facial expression well. Something was going on. I asked several questions with limited response. "I'll tell you when we get home."

"Home?! I thought we were going to the dentist!"

As we walked to the school gate, I saw our car. This must be serious. Dad was on nights and would usually be asleep at this time. Thoughts were jumping through my head on the way home, feeling sick and on the edge of tears.

"Why won't you tell me what's going on?!"

Mum was a worrier, but Dad—he was sensible and always at work. Never a tag team. This must be big! Was my sister dead? Did something happen to one of the dogs? Maybe the dogs got into the gerbil cage and killed Misty! Perhaps they choked on Misty, and now they're all dead? Did I not press the buttons on my TV in the correct sequence last night? Was this all my fault?

We walked into the living room.

[Woody] LOCK THE DOOR!

[Me] Not now, mate, I might need to escape.

I sat down on the sofa. Dad was standing up, looking at the floor. Mum was kneeling on the floor in front of me, crying.

She produced a bag of a powdery grey substance with small lumps in it. Mum had been "tidying" my room—parent-speak for a forensic fingertip search.

Stumbling across what she thought was my secret stash of crack, she'd been on the phone with FRANK—the drugs helpline for over an hour that morning. Despite the counsellor telling my mum that, based on her description of an anxious nerdy teen, who spent more time in the house with his head in medical journals than playing out with his friends, there were no apparent signs. The professional advice was to speak openly and calmly about it with me when I got home from school. Unfortunately, they'd never met my mother before. She didn't tolerate uncertainty well. They failed to clarify that "when I was home" didn't mean taking me out of school the second she put the phone down.

[Mum] WHAT'S THIS?! (clutching the bag in her hand)
[Me] What's what? (trying to see what it is)
[Mum] ARE YOU DOING DRUGS?!
[Me] Wha. . .What?! No!
[Mum] WHAT'S THIS THEN?! (shaking the bag)
[Me] (realising). . . It's Misty's.
[Mum] WHAT IS MISS-TISS? IS IT DRUGS?!
[Me] WHY HAVE YOU BEEN IN MY ROOM?!

[Mum] I WAS TIDYING!

[Me] STOP GOING IN MY ROOM!

[Mum] WHAT–IS–MISS-TISS?! (shaking the bag)

[Me] M–I–S–T–Y. Misty. The gerbil. It's gerbil food.

[Dad] (shaking his head) I'm off to bed!

[Mum] Misty has pellets–this is powder. Where's it from?

[Me] Hampsons pet shop. It's new. Bloke said it's better.

[Mum] (penny drops, now uncontrollably laughing)

[Me] FOR FUCK'S SAKE!

[Mum] WHAT HAVE I SAID ABOUT SWEARING!

On the plus side, it got me out of maths and my most dreaded lesson of the week—PE. While I was a worried-well teenager, I was also a savvy opportunist and attempted to emotionally blackmail her. I would need to have the following day off school as well to recover from the trauma of my emergency dental work. Adding weight to the lie she told the school.

She was having none of it.

As an adult, I'm now more aware of the magnitude of pressure and fear parents experience with their teens, particularly around drugs and substance use. Although my mum admits that her reaction was over the top at the time, disproportionate to the context, this was also a time when class-A drugs were filtering into our local community. They appeared out of nowhere and were rising exponentially.

The uptake from young customers didn't discriminate by income, status, or school. Many teenagers were being collected for *emergency dental appointments* from the private grammar school up the road. The only difference was that they were driven home in a Range Rover rather than a Ford Sierra. It was rife and wrecking young people's lives and families.

By the time I was eighteen, a few of the popular kids I attended high school with were either hooked on serious drugs, in prison, or dead. I was one of the lucky ones who managed to avoid its clutches. Not because I was a saint. My parents were in the middle of a divorce, and I was partying heavily, making up for all the lost time at school. I was offered hard drugs on several occasions. Teenage brains are curious—I was tempted.

But, there was a story on the BBC about a young person who died the first time they took heroin.

I also knew from the medical books that the effects of amphetamine, opioids, and cocaine included rotten skin and teeth, cartilage wasting of the septum, liver and kidney function problems, and heart arrhythmia.

There was absolutely no way I was doing that!

4

Thought Crimes

W hy do we believe in monsters despite the facts?

In 1921, a Swiss psychiatrist named Hermann Rorschach began showing his patients a series of inkblot images.

"What might this be?"

There was no correct answer. This was a test to see what his patients would project, and where their minds would go when faced with the ambiguity and uncertainty of the shapeless, undefined, symmetrical inkblots. Would they lean into darker parts? Perhaps there would be familiar patterns, creating ideas and images where none were to be found.

A century later, the Rorschach inkblot test is still famous.[1] Many will associate the images with Hollywood depictions of psychology and psychiatry in film. Yet, they are far less commonly used in modern clinical practice, at least in the UK. They are also considered a little outdated and unscientific by today's standards. Nevertheless, it's a helpful way to think about intrusive thoughts.

You will recognise test card V from the cover of this book. Most people report seeing a bat, a moth, or a butterfly.

Test Card V (Rorschach, 1921)

Card VI, on the other hand, tends to be where things start to become more nuanced. What do you see?

Test Card VI (Rorschach, 1921)

A rug? A fur coat and hat? A sword slicing through stone? Squashed fruit? Perhaps you're someone who has a tendency to focus on the physical body: a flesh wound or sexual organs. Possibly more contamination led: microorganisms, bacteria, viruses. What about parasites? Insects? Aliens?

Of course, for the pragmatists and thought-avoiders who quickly skipped the page, it's simply a blob of ink on folded paper. Still, a crude demonstration of how human minds work.

Our brains take in information from our surroundings and try to make sense of it based on our points of reference, whether recent or from the past. Interpretations vary wildly, and we will all have different emotional responses. Some will have no feelings about it; others may experience excitement, interest, and possibly negative emotions, such as disgust and repulsion. There will also be those of you who feel dismissive, lacking interest, bored to tears, and wondering when the paragraph will eventually end.

The bottom line?

If random blots of ink can evoke different thoughts and emotions, imagine what can happen when our minds show us realistic images and mental movies that send our nervous system into overdrive.

Some people dismiss the thoughts and images as nonsense, having little to no reaction. Someone with OCD can be catapulted through court, skip the judge and jury and bang themselves to rights in a category A prison before they have a chance to protest.

Our brains are hard-wired to pay attention to threats, and if our darker thoughts evoke fear and anxiety, we are more likely to start paying attention to them. Anyone familiar with CBT will likely have encountered the thought suppression test.

"Don't think about a white bear!"[2]

This staple technique demonstrates that the more we try to avoid or not think about distressing or anxiety-inducing thoughts, the more they return, like a boomerang.

And you don't need a white bear to try it out. Let's go for something more provocative.

Spend a bit of time looking at the image of the handcuffs. Then, for thirty seconds, close your eyes.

DO NOT think about handcuffs!

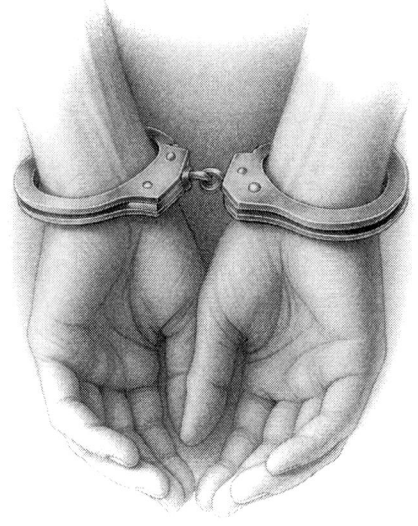

＊ ＊ ＊

So, remember little four-year-old Toby and his escapades at the supermarket? Well, it's now the start of the school year in 2003, and he is fourteen years old.

During the end of last term, he struggled to attend due to anxiety; his grades were dropping, and he was becoming withdrawn. His mother and stepfather had sourced a private therapist; they told Toby's parents that he was making superficial cuts to his skin with a compass due to struggling with all the changes going on at home.

His biological father moved to Spain, his ten-year-old brother was experiencing behavioural difficulties due to a neurological condition, and his new baby sister had just arrived. They had been given some tips and tricks to work together as a family. Toby wasn't at all happy; it had upset his mum. He no longer trusted the therapist, so he told them he was feeling a lot better and didn't need to continue.

Yet, he was still constantly disinfecting the work surfaces in his bedroom with bacterial wipes and mentally counting in his head. But the physical symptoms of anxiety had settled down quite a bit over the summer holidays, managing to get out more and spending time with his best friend.

Toby is now sitting in a history class watching an episode from a TV drama series about the Tudors. As was common in 15th - 18th century Britain, it depicts the general public cheering as people have their heads chopped off, are stoned to death, and women are burned alive at the stake, accused of being witches. None of this bothers Toby—it's just TV.

The acting is a bit crap, and he starts glancing around the classroom. His attention is drawn to the maturing bodies of other fourteen-year-olds.

A classmate becomes aware that Toby is staring at them. They silently mouth "paedo" at him and then whispers to the person sitting beside them. Immediately embarrassed, Toby's face flushes red. His attention snaps back to the Tudors just as the camera zooms in for a close-up of baby Elizabeth I in the arms of Anne Boleyn. Toby is now anxious and awkwardly trying to hide an erection underneath the desk.

What's wrong with this picture?

Nothing—a typical teenager!

As reasonable adults, we wouldn't leap to the conclusion that Toby has a fetish for the Tudors. We know that from the timeline described, his physical body is responding naturally to the stimulus of his peers in the classroom.

If Toby then masturbates alone at home while thinking about the bodies of other fourteen-year-olds, we wouldn't accuse him of being a sexual predator. This is all within the normal parameters for Toby's age and developmental stage.

So why does he start worrying about being a paedophile?

Well, that was Elizabeth I. Not the monarch—the mental image of the baby playing her in the badly acted drama. This image popped into his head while watching regular porn that evening. Since then, every time Toby masturbates, intrusive images of babies arrive, becoming more graphic and distressing.

He starts experimenting to prove to himself that he is not attracted to young children—constant monitoring, checking, purposely thinking about young children and observing his physical body for signs of arousal. During a TV advert for baby formula, he sneaks off to the bathroom to check. He inspects his bedsheets every morning.

"Was I dreaming about children?"

Obviously, hyper-focussing on your genitals is likely to lead to sexual arousal, especially if you are a teenager. Mainly as a result of all the poking and prodding, but it starts to feed the bias of Toby's intrusive thoughts.

"If this is happening, then I really MUST be a paedophile!"

Paranoid thoughts then start to surface about the PornHub searches on his mobile phone while his parents were doing their Saturday shop at the supermarket.

"Were any of them underage?"

During a regular Google search, Toby now learns that the age of criminal responsibility in the UK is ten years old, and fourteen-year-olds can be imprisoned for serious crimes. His search history is now even more evidence of guilt if a case is brought to court, and they might even implicate his brother—he's ten.

Finally, Toby puts himself before his personal judge and jury—guilty as charged! He starts mentally preparing for what life would be like behind bars, alone.

Toby doesn't want to bother his mother; she already has much to handle. He doesn't want to speak to his stepfather—he'll send him back to therapy. So he calls his dad in Spain. "You're being ridiculous! Stop watching porn, it's bad for you!" He is anxious to tell anyone about it at school; he has already been picked on and doesn't want to risk telling his best friend about it.

Toby feels isolated. He avoids sexual thoughts and arousal as much as possible. His compulsions escalate, and he starts self-harming as a temporary way to manage his thoughts.

Like health-focused intrusions, Toby has developed a hyper-focus on the physical body, including bodily sensations. The difference is the addition of the natural urges and stimulation that are getting caught up in the crossfire. Essentially, this is not as simple as thought-feelings-actions; it's a tightly wound additional mix of biological processes creating a confirmatory feedback loop.

But for some, no matter how much psychological education is understood, regardless of how much their mind joins the dots between fact and fiction, and despite very in-depth and frank explanations about the biological processes involved in the natural human body, they continue to loop.

* * *

But why do we have horrid thoughts in the first place if we really don't want them? Are they truly all smoke with no fire?

What can be challenging to think about is that humans have a darker side to our psyche. Not convinced? Do a quick search on Google for popular mainstream novel and movie genres. Sex, violence, crime and horror. It's a multi-billion-dollar industry.

For many decades, psychoanalytic therapists have considered the human mind to be full of conflicts, contradictions, impulses and drives. Freud referred to this as a tension between our instincts and desires (the *id*) and the moralistic, idealistic, critical parts of our mind (the *superego*). For those of us with a tendency toward obsession and compulsion, this rugby scrum is moderated by an anxious and often burdened referee— the *ego*.[3]

It's only in the past few decades that the field of psychology and psychotherapy has shifted its focus toward positive thinking and the solution-focused approaches of popular psychology.

Yet, anyone working as a trauma therapist, particularly those using approaches such as psychodynamic therapy or EMDR, will be very familiar with the violent and graphic fantasies that can often emerge.

In cases of chronic abuse, this commonly involves helping someone to move from a state of powerlessness toward feeling more in control. Patients are sometimes encouraged to use imagery to help them end their suffering. At times, these themes include violence against the perpetrator, in their mind.

It's also common to encounter suppressed anger and rage that maintains depression. Many people encounter violent acts in fantasy, including graphic sexual thoughts and images that they would rarely, if ever, think about in their typical day-to-day.

In the majority of cases, they are ego-dystonic, whether they have OCD or not.

Allowing these to play out in the confidence of a therapy room can act as a bridge to more deeply rooted painful memories and implicit feelings—unrelated to the explicit content of the fantasy. The mind simply needs to do something with the feelings that are being elicited to help bring them to a resolution.

This doesn't mean overly interpreting nonsensical intrusive thoughts; with OCD, it's more about taking the intrusive thoughts to their conclusion. "If you were sent to prison for your thought crimes, what would that mean about you, now?"

So we get curious about the generated emotions. "Noticing what's happening in your body as you tell me that; what's your earliest memory of that feeling?"

These are typical clients in a typical clinic. Ordinary people leading regular lives. Most have no history of violence, and that's highly unlikely to change.

This was the case for Rosa a fifty-nine-year-old office worker, seeing a psychologist for the first time. She was referred for brief, time-limited therapy due to workplace stress and had up to ten sessions funded through occupational health to support her return to work.

Rosa has worked for the same firm for over thirty years as a PA to one of the directors. Following a merger with a larger firm, her role changed. Her new line manager is half her age and less experienced and changed the policies and procedures that Rosa was instrumental in creating. Now, with reduced responsibility and learning an entirely new system, she asks to meet with her old boss, but he isn't interested in discussing it.

Rosa wasn't sleeping well, having days where she couldn't get out of bed, let alone go to work. She didn't know what was happening. Initially, she thought that she might be anaemic, but her blood tests were all normal. She had no prior problems with her mental health. Still happily married, always committed to extensive charitable work with her local church group, and adores her three grandchildren.

"What do I have to be depressed about?!"

She would arrive for sessions immaculately dressed and constantly smiling but didn't take well to exploring the past.

"I had an amazing childhood."

Numerous references to her work achievements over the years are made, but any attempt to explore her current difficulties at work would be dismissed or redirected.

After a few weeks of our dialectical dance, marked by a lot of smiling but little traction with the "Tips and tricks to help me get my mojo back," we eventually land on murderous rage.

Years of devoted service, all in the endless but pointless pursuit of being noticed and respected. Now, feeling overlooked and taken for granted.

"They've thrown me aside like TRASH!"

During the anger protocol (it's a thing in EMDR), Rosa can finally feel the location of anger in her body, rising like molten lava from her hips. Pressure behind her head, tightness in her chest, now rapidly tapping from side to side in a butterfly hug.

[Rosa] I WANT TO BASH HIS ARROGANT HEAD IN.

[Me] Notice where you feel that in your body.

[Rosa] AND SHOVE THAT TROPHY HE KEEPS ON
    HIS DESK RIGHT UP HIS AR—

[Me] —Aaaannd notice.

Rosa's depression lifts, and she goes back to her charitable work with the church. Now, she is spending quality time with her grandkids again and eventually lands herself a pay rise with a new company. No one is wounded during the process, apart from the imagined ego of her former boss.

— ⁕ —

Violent, sexual, or morally disturbing thoughts are amongst the most common with OCD, at least in my experience. In each case, these have been ego-dystonic.

The man who fears crashing his car into people anxiously reviews dashcam footage for hours. The woman who fears she might touch a child inappropriately avoids her own niece. These aren't people on the edge of offending; they're doing everything possible to prevent and undo what their mind shows them.

However, this doesn't simply imply that someone who has OCD is incapable of terrible things. Obsessive and compulsive traits are not exclusive to law-abiding and prosocial people. Yet, there is an essential distinction between actions and intentions versus thoughts and images.

There are published studies reporting cases of OCD in samples of convicted sex offenders, including child sex offences.[4]

—Okay, let's pause there.

If that sentence has just sent you catapulting to the roof with a massive spike of anxiety, your mind has very likely just quickly mashed the terms *OCD* and *sex offender*. Quite possible that you missed the bit about actions versus thoughts.

Hear me out.

There is a wide range of OCD subtypes, such as contamination-based fears. Child sex offences typically involve actions consistent with paedophilic behaviour, intentionally grooming children, efforts to conceal, and poor insight into the harm and damage being caused to others, not excessive cleansing and washing in response to thoughts about contamination.

The *Risk Assessment and Management Guidance for OCD* published in 2009 found no documented cases where someone with OCD had acted on their ego-dystonic thoughts.[5] I've intensively trawled the databases of clinical and forensic journals for cases while researching for this book. I came up empty handed as well. Albeit with the odd fleeting intrusive worry that my searches might be flagged to INTERPOL.

Essentially, it is possible that someone can have an OCD diagnosis AND reside in a forensic setting. However, with people who have sexual tendencies toward young people, this is evidenced by explicit intentions and actions. Not anxiety-based avoidant behaviour due to distressing images and thoughts about children.

Even those of us with obsessive-compulsive personality traits, who spend our lives in the relentless pursuit of being a perfect human, have no greater moral immunity.

There are well-documented serial killers with perfectionistic tendencies, including ritualistic compulsions.

"Modus Operandi."

Take Dennis Rader, infamously known as BTK.

Bind them.

Torture them.

Kill them.

Rader's sociopathic obsession with control and dominance led to a series of grotesque murders, each meticulously planned and executed. His nickname summed up his methodical approach. Compulsive and ritualistic binding of his victims and precise and careful documentation of his crimes. He also could compartmentalise his actions with an outward persona: a church leader and family man, hiding in plain sight.

But Rader's actions went way beyond those of clinical perfectionism; he had extreme tendencies for sadism and malignant narcissism. He derived pleasure from his power over his victims, their fear and suffering. He sent letters to the police and media, perverse pride —a grandiose sense of self.

While the United States houses the highest concentration of documented serial killers, we've also had a few homegrown in the UK—literally fifty miles from my office.

Myra Hindley and Ian Brady, the infamous Moors Murderers, shared similar traits with Rader but with the added twist of a partnership. Brady's sadistic paedophilic fantasies found a willing participant in Hindley. A toxic dynamic amplified their actions. They fed from each other's desires for power and control over their victims. They also recorded their victims during the murders.

For Rader, Brady, and Hindley, these cases were fuelled by sexual gratification—not fear. For Rader, the sexual component was linked to the act of binding and torturing. With Brady and Hindley, this also extended to further torturing the families of the victims, manipulating them, throwing red herrings, and withholding information about where the children were buried on the moors.

Winnie Johnson, the mother of Keith Bennett, one of Brady and Hindley's victims, relentlessly appealed to Brady for information about her son while he was incarcerated. Sadly, she died in August 2012, having never been able to bring home her son's remains.

All horrific, wicked, and terribly sad.

So, for anyone reading this who has OCD and experiences violent or sexually intrusive obsessions.

Do you honestly see yourself in these examples?

Really, be honest with yourself. At all?

Is it starting to make sense why any clinician experienced with OCD still hasn't called the police or social services when you rock up for your tenth session?

I mean, you'll undoubtedly have some horrid images in your head, but what about your intentions and actions? Anywhere near Rader, Brady, or Hindley?

I'm going to assume that it's highly unlikely.

So that should be that, then!

Cured!

If only, eh?

Many people I've worked with, whether teenagers or adults, experience more covert cognitive compulsions—mentally reviewing "what if" retrospective acts. They will go into their deep mind web, data mining for flaws and inconsistencies, punching holes in theories. Going up mental side streets and slithering around roadblocks.

"Did I carry out those actions, but I don't remember doing it?! Perhaps a dissociative memory gap?"

Here's the heads-up to save another blood pressure spike.

—No!

Dissociation can range from mild to moderate symptoms, such as emotional detachment, feelings of things being unreal, or depersonalisation. This is common with anxiety and phobia-based problems. I used to get this every time I visited the GP or dentist.

It can sometimes be more severe, such as flashbacks, zoning out and emotional numbing, typical of PTSD and complex trauma. In extreme cases, such as dissociative identity disorder (DID), dissociation can result in the development of distinct identity states or *alters*. These can be markedly different in age, gender, tone of voice, accent, and behaviour, sometimes presenting with childlike characteristics.

Each state typically forms in response to trauma, taking on specific roles to help the person to manage overwhelming experiences. Transitions between alters can cause confusion, memory loss, and disruptions in the person's sense of self, leading to noticeable gaps in awareness and identity.[6]

This is not OCD!

As a condition, DID is much less common, and, similar to people who experience psychosis, they are typically more at risk of harm from others than toward others.

If you're tempted to hit Google—I've saved you the trouble. There are rare but highly publicised cases where people have claimed to commit serious crimes, sometimes murder, without any memory of doing so.

Billy Milligan is perhaps the most well-known example of someone found *not guilty* of serious crimes on the grounds of dissociative identity disorder. In the 1970s, he was arrested for multiple rapes in Ohio. During psychiatric evaluations, Milligan was found to have numerous alters, including a Yugoslav man, a young girl, and a teacher.

According to clinicians, these alters committed the crimes while Milligan himself, his original personality, was unaware. The court accepted the diagnosis, and he became the first person in U.S. history to be acquitted of major crimes using a DID defence.[7] Milligan wasn't a serial killer, but his case is frequently cited in discussions about whether someone could harm others and have no recollection of it.

Then there was Kenneth Bianchi, one of the so-called Hillside Stranglers, who, along with his cousin, murdered several women in California in the late 1970s. After being arrested, Bianchi claimed he had DID and that one of his alters had committed the murders.

Unlike Milligan, his story didn't hold up under scrutiny. Experts found inconsistencies in his behaviour and eventually concluded he was feigning the condition.[8] Bianchi was convicted and sentenced to life in prison. His case shows how dissociation can be misused or exaggerated in criminal proceedings, especially when the stakes are high.

A more ambiguous case is that of Ed Gein, whose crimes inspired fictional characters like Norman Bates and Buffalo Bill. Gein wasn't technically a serial killer, but was linked to two murders, but what made his story infamous was what he did with the bodies.

He exhumed corpses, crafted trophies from human remains, and lived in a house filled with body parts.[9]

Psychiatrists at the time described him as deeply disturbed and disconnected from reality. While he wasn't diagnosed with DID, there were clear signs of dissociation, including a blurring of realities. Gein was eventually declared legally insane and spent the rest of his life in psychiatric care.

But again, the key distinction here is that DID and OCD are not the same.

For someone with DID, losing time or being unaware of their actions is part of the condition.

By contrast, people with OCD *do not* have alternate identity states, and with the exception of occasional zoning out due to anxiety, they *don't* lose time in the same way.

The fear of having done something terrible is usually not based on missing time—it's based on doubt. Not feeling *certain enough* that something didn't happen, and set off in the pursuit of reassurance. The mind then fills in the blanks with bottomless disturbing possibilities. "What if I ran someone over and didn't notice?" "What if I touched that child on the bus and just forgot?" "What if I killed someone and blocked it out?"

This is not amnesia, it's just a bunch of hypothetical crap that strips you of autonomy, healthy choices and decisions.

So yes, there are cases of people claiming to have committed serious crimes without memory of doing so. In a very small number of instances, those claims are supported by complex dissociative conditions. But these are extremely rare, and even then, the clinical picture is very different from OCD.

It's cruel, really.

Yet, there is a big difference between *what-IF* and *what-IS*. The former is hypothetical situations that, by their nature, have no tangible solution. You can't solve a problem that doesn't exist. The latter is what has actually taken place, a current issue grounded in more objective facts.

Of course, holding conflicting ideas at once can be difficult to do. Many of us don't wander through life constantly thinking about our universally human capacity to occasionally have dark or immoral thoughts AND still be decent, caring people.

Most tend to live it. A given.

Although the intrusive thoughts generated by OCD are often unpleasant, they usually latch onto existing internal narratives. If a person already holds the core belief "I am bad," intrusive thoughts about harming someone or committing an immoral act become more than just passing mental noise. They raise the threat level and become confirmatory.

"If I *think* this, then I *really must* be bad!"

But what actions are you guilty of, exactly?

The most common thing folk with OCD are typically guilty of is placing a metaphorical electronic tag on their own ankles. Attending work, seeing friends, watching the kids in their Christmas play, going on holiday, all with the feeling of being out on license or under surveillance, percolating away at the back of your mind. Anxiously awaiting arrest at any moment for your thought crimes.

But at what cost?

For how long?

5

Original Sins

If I could believe that God was not angry with me, I would stand on my head for joy

—Martin Luther

E ven saints have their critics.

Mother Teresa, born Anjezë Gonxhe Bojaxhiu in 1910 in what is now Skopje, North Macedonia, was a Catholic nun and missionary best known for her work with the poor and dying in Kolkata, India. She founded the *Missionaries of Charity* in 1950, dedicating her life to serving society's most vulnerable. Public perception of Mother Teresa is generally one of admiration, often seen as a shining symbol of compassion, humility, and selfless service. She remains a widely respected figure and was canonised by the Catholic Church on September 4th 2016, as *Saint Teresa of Calcutta*.

Yet, she was the subject of one of the most scathing takedowns in modern religious history, led by journalist Christopher Hitchens.

In his book *The Missionary Position* and the Channel Four documentary *Hell's Angel*, Hitchens painted her not as a saint but as a reactionary. A "fanatic, fundamentalist, and fraud" who built a global reputation by romanticising suffering rather than relieving it.[1][2] He accused her of running hospices that denied basic medical care, instead preaching that "suffering is a gift from God," and claimed she was "a friend of poverty" rather than the poor.[3]

Far from being politically neutral, he implied that she accepted donations from fraudsters like Charles Keating, praised brutal regimes like the Duvaliers in Haiti, and used her platform to spread the Catholic Church's most hardline stances on abortion, contraception, and divorce. In Hitchens' view, she was "a servant of earthly powers," cloaked in sanctimony and fuelled by an unquestioning global media.[4]

However, his target wasn't just Mother Teresa; it was a broad critique of the cultural immunity granted to moral authority wrapped in religious language and good intentions. The image of a woman dedicating her life to people experiencing poverty in the most deprived areas of Kolkata can feel comforting. It can also relieve us of thinking about the more complex questions around suffering, political systems, and our own actions and inaction.

For some people, morality and virtue aren't just tied to cultural performance or public expectation. Extreme perceptions invade their thoughts and distort their conscience, turning even the simple act of sitting down to eat an evening meal into an ethical landmine.

This is referred to in OCD terms as *scrupulosity*: a form of obsessional doubt that latches onto religion, morality, or personal integrity.

People can experience intrusive thoughts that they have sinned, had blasphemous thoughts, or acted immorally, even in minor or imagined ways. In most cases, accompanied by intense guilt, fear of eternal punishment, or anxiety about having violated deeply held values.

In religious contexts, scrupulosity can manifest as compulsive prayer, or an overwhelming need to precisely follow religious rituals. These are not necessarily expressions of the devout—in many cases, they don't map onto the person's existing faith or cultural practices. For example, people with prior agnostic or atheistic beliefs start to fear that they're offending God, Allah, or other deities.

Compulsions might include confessing multiple times daily, avoiding places or people that feel *impure*, or engaging in internal debates. This can be highly distressing, particularly where someone *is* part of a religious community where their compulsions might be considered *atypical practices*, potentially leading to further thoughts of blasphemy or offence.

As with other subtypes of OCD, these can get tangled up with the natural physiological responses of the body.

A case study recently published by Engin Büyüköksüz documents the clinical treatment of a young person in their late adolescence experiencing recurring intrusive sexual thoughts about male religious figures while masturbating.[5] This was causing intense feelings of guilt and shame, resulting in significant psychological distress. The young person had also started interrupting themselves to prevent ejaculation. "An unforgivable sin."

This would lead to avoidance of masturbation and creating elaborate, punishing thoughts about their family members to neutralise the perceived wrongdoing.

Where they had managed to successfully ejaculate, this would then generate intrusive thoughts about their semen contaminating underwear, school equipment, and household surfaces such as worktops, leading to extensive cleansing rituals: excessive showering and washing routines following sexual arousal. However, the fear wasn't necessarily about physical cleanliness but of moral or spiritual contamination, driven by the belief that sexual thoughts involving religious figures had rendered these objects impure.

While I found this fascinating to read about from a clinical perspective, having worked with similar cases, it also made me feel incredibly sad. It must be a horrible way to experience life as an adult, let alone as a teenager.

Scrupulosity is not a modern invention. Way before psychologists started faffing about with the terms, the phenomenon was experientially lived—most famously by Martin Luther, a 16th-century monk.

Luther was consumed by an unrelenting fear that he was morally corrupt and unforgivable in the eyes of God. He confessed excessively, sometimes for hours at a time, returning moments later in case he had missed a single sin. He agonised over intrusive blasphemous thoughts and described being tormented by what he called *Anfechtung*—a state of spiritual despair and self-condemnation.[6] Luther was unable to feel assured of grace, even when doctrine allowed it. His internal crisis eventually catalysed a break from the Catholic Church. The psychological features of his torment, persistent doubt, moral perfectionism, intrusive obsession and compulsive rituals are pretty recognisable.

People can also experience secular themes, such as the fear of being unethical, harmful, or fundamentally "bad". While there is less worry about offending God, people are afraid of violating an internal moral or ethical code. Content can vary wildly.

Some people fear they've lied without realising it. Others may obsess over whether a facial expression was deceptive or manipulative. There can also be a fixation on causing emotional harm—accidentally offending someone, crossing a boundary, or being perceived as exploitative. Sometimes, this can also manifest within intimate relationships, questioning their own or their partner's morality.

Certainly, here in the UK and the US, there has been a significant increase in people taking to social media to share personal ideas and values that divide public opinion. Scrupulosity can leak into more progressive or identity-based themes, dietary choices, or mentally reviewing conversations for any sign of unconscious bias or offensive language.

This is not to be confused with personal lifestyle choices or our collective social conscience to ensure we look after each other and the planet. It is typically much more extreme in nature, in the ongoing pursuit of "doing the right thing".

But what exactly is sin?

How might one end up in Hell?

It depends on what you're reading, really.

Dante Alighieri mapped out Hell poetically in his 14th-century epic *The Divine Comedy*. The first volume, *Inferno,* takes you on a guided tour.[7] It's impressively structured. There are different levels of sin, and each punishment has a purpose, with a single guiding principle.

Sin is a distortion of *love*.

Dante's version of Hell is divided into nine circles, descending as the sins grow more intentional and morally corrupt. The framework is grounded in medieval Catholicism and the philosophy of St. Augustine and Thomas Aquinas, who believed that all moral failure stems from *disordered* love.[8]

To love the wrong thing, or the right thing in the wrong way, would be to turn away from reason, virtue, and ultimately, turning away from God.

The sins in the upper circles, *limbo, lust, gluttony, greed,* and *wrath,* are viewed as failures of self-restraint, human weaknesses, and lapses of control, what Dante refers to as *incontinence.* Although severe punishment is not yet damnable in the deepest sense. The real descent begins with *heresy,* then moves to *violence, fraud,* and *treachery*—the betrayal of trust. The bottom tier is encased in ice, where Satan lies frozen. For Dante, betrayal is not just sinful but the unravelling of all moral and social order.

What distinguishes each level is not necessarily the sinful act itself but the intention behind it. The deeper the sin, the more deliberate and calculated it is.

Deeper circles punish premeditation, such as those who deceive, manipulate, or destroy out of conscious choice. These are the gravest sins, not committed through loss of emotional control, but in calculated, detached clarity.

The punishments are a form of moral symbolism known as *contrapasso,* meaning "suffer the opposite" or "counter-suffering." The punishment mirrors the sin. The lustful are faced with strong, biting winds, reflecting their lack of control. The gluttonous lie in filth under icy cold rain, symbolising their mindless consumption. Fraudsters wear cloaks lined with lead, beautiful on the outside but crushing them inside. Each punishment is not about inflicting pain but revealing the true nature of the soul.[9]

There is some thematic overlap with the Seven Deadly Sins.[10] However, Dante's moral schema is more nuanced. Sins of impulse are less severe than sins of betrayal; moral weakness is not the same as malice, and so on.

Ultimately, the concept is not about breaking rules; it's about breaking the relationship with yourself, with others, and with the divine. Hell, in this sense, is not a prison; rather, it mirrors the soul's trajectory. You become what you love. You suffer as you sinned. You dwell where your will has led.

Granted, I'm not a theologian, but from what I understand, the idea of sin runs through many religious traditions, but the concepts vary quite a bit.

In Christianity, it's often a rupture in the relationship with God.[11] In Judaism, more about *missing the mark*—something potentially correctable.[12] Islam tends to emphasise personal responsibility, distinguishing between major and minor forms, and denies the concept of inherited guilt.[13] In Hinduism and Buddhism, sin isn't framed as an offence but as a karmic imbalance or unskilful action.[14] What broadly unites the concepts is the view that moral failure includes relationships with others and the wider world.

While there are commonly held values: following the law of the land, trying to treat people as you would wish to be treated yourself, morality, more broadly, has never been static. Many religious doctrines were shaped by social and political conditions. Some were practical tools for governance or hygiene.

But moral codes, similar to languages, evolve. And where and when you are born often determines which ones you inherit.

DANTE'S INFERNO

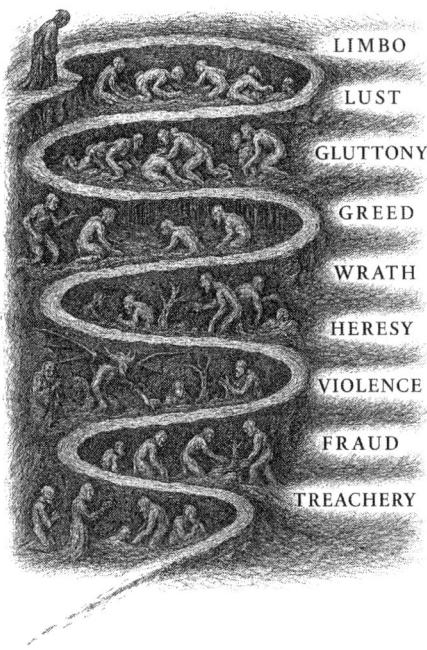

Before I go any further, it's important to point out that religion, faith, and spirituality are still incredibly important to many people in contemporary society. For some, faith goes way further in their daily lives than any psychotherapy I could offer as a psychologist. I respect that. Just hold in mind this is a chapter about scrupulosity, and I'm being intentionally provocative for reasons that will hopefully become clear.

—Gird your loins.

Many people discover religion or faith in adulthood, making conscious and informed choices, sometimes as a result of profound, unexplainable experiences. Yet, it's also fair to say that many of us were born into conditions that shaped our beliefs, including concepts of sin and morality.

Had I arrived in the world in a different time and place—part of the Diné (Navajo) Nation in North America, I would have been welcomed into the community through traditional rites that recognised individual identity and spiritual role. Possibly marked by a naming ceremony.

Within many Native American traditions, gender was not seen as binary or tightly policed. I would have likely grown up understanding the concept of *Two-Spirit* people who embody combined genders, often celebrated, holding ceremonial roles in their communities. [15]

The existence of fluid gender identity was not a threat to social order; it was an accepted variation within it. The dominance of traditions and concepts in North America seen today, arrived with colonisation and forced conversion when European Christian norms were imposed and Indigenous ritual traditions were suppressed.

In ancient Rome, powerful men often engaged in sexual relationships with other men, usually male adolescents or slaves. Morality wasn't about the gender of each sexual partner but the status and position of each person.[16] From today's perspective, we may have a multitude of moral and ethical considerations regarding consent and power dynamics. But at the time, these were established practices in both the public and private lives of Rome's elite.

Even further back, Greek mythology placed desire in the divine realm.[17] The gods themselves were depicted as sexually fluid, morally inconsistent, and often predatory.

But I wasn't raised during the times of ancient Rome, nor belonged to the Navajo. I was born to a white British family in Yorkshire, England. I developed schemas around binary concepts of gender, where the local dialect included derogatory slurs for any deviation from heterosexuality. In keeping with the typical cultural traditions and norms of the time and place, I was also christened into the Church of England as a baby.

This is an institution established by King Henry VIII in 1534 following a break from the Roman Catholic Church, and it caused a kerfuffle for quite a bit of time afterwards.

By the time King James I took the throne in England (1603-1625), there were growing tensions and political challenges: religious division between Puritans and Anglicans and ongoing issues with Catholic Europe. He needed a way to unify religious factions and consolidate his authority. In 1604, along with scholarly translators, he set about tinkering with the sacred texts. The King James Bible is still the most commonly distributed version in mainstream circulation to this day.

Yet, modern scholars have pointed to revisions that were made, such as Leviticus 18:22 and 20:13.[18] These were translated with emphasis on homosexual relationships as "abomination". Earlier texts, including the Latin Vulgate and some Talmudic interpretations, did not frame these passages in the same way. Some historians argue that prior renderings were more likely aimed at exploitative sexual practices, including those involving minors or ritual abuse, rather than consensual adult relationships. It was also rumoured at the time that King James himself was conflicted about his own sexual identity.[19]

Either way, it gave powerful fuel to moral condemnation of homosexuality, embedding centuries of stigma and theological justification that has been weaponised in the pursuit of persecution for centuries.[20] This has included young people being ostracised by their families. People fleeing their country of origin due to fear of punishment by death. It gave way to abhorrent psychological practices, so-called "conversion therapy"—aversive attempts at behavioural modification that, in most cases, led to poor mental health and suicide.

Homosexuality was first partially decriminalised in England and Wales by the Sexual Offences Act 1967, which legalised consensual sexual acts between two men over the age of twenty-one, provided the acts occurred in private. Up until that point, sexual contact between consenting gay men would lead to imprisonment or a psychiatric treatment order.

It wasn't until 1973 that homosexuality was declassified as a mental illness in the revision of the Diagnostic and Statistical Manual. However, due to the privacy clause in the law, even if there was an unrelated third party present in another room of the house, this would render the consensual act illegal. Prosecutions of gay men continued for decades after 1967 under charges such as gross and public indecency.

These are not isolated examples. Throughout history, religious texts have been edited, redacted, and reinterpreted in various ways to serve the strategic interests of people in positions of power. Theological concepts were frequently adapted to reinforce civil law and support national identity and social hierarchies. In some cases, verses were weaponised to criminalise entire groups of people or to preserve roles that served patriarchal or colonial agendas. These were decisions made by mortal humans, often behind closed doors, with motives that were, at times, more political than spiritual.

While morality has been heavily influenced by monarchs, gods, and scripture, in modern society, we also have access to the wider world in a way that would have been unthinkable, even when I was a child. Yet, the boundaries of what each of us considers morally offensive are still wildly unstable.

One person is enraged by a drag queen reading to children in a library; another is appalled by Christian prayer in a secular school. A TikTok video of a woman breastfeeding is championed as empowering—the next person to comment pulls her apart, calling her obscene.

Famous figures use their large public platforms to share their opinion on current issues. Once adored by many, now sitting in the bin of terrible things.

Cancel culture.

Lots of people are finding it tough to keep up with changes to familiar terminology and rapid shifts to established norms.

Racism, war, abuse, violence, global warming, and children still dying from poverty and lack of healthcare. Billionaires divide communities through strategic moral and ethical panic.

Many are disenfranchised.

It would be easy to think that the world had simply gone to shit all of a sudden—but it's been going on for millennia. If Dante's version of Hell truly exists, there's going to be a seriously long waiting list.

In a world this contradictory, it's not surprising that people start looking inward and begin beating themselves up.

So, how do we help people with scrupulosity OCD in the midst of all that?

Given that psychologists are typically not religious experts and we are not the authority on morality, we simply go about it as we would with any other form of OCD. However, while most people who experience obsession and compulsion often recognise their fear as irrational or exaggerated, it can be challenging to overcome.

From my own clinical perspective, there is much greater scope to directly challenge the belief that someone will contaminate and accidentally kill their entire family from touching a clean toilet seat. With careful encouragement, the therapist and the client can physically shove their hands in the lavatory (exposure), tolerate their feelings while not washing their hands (response prevention), and place bets on whose family will be wiped out first—no one dies as a result.

Yet, challenging the possibility of eternal damnation from the wrath of an unforgiving God? Whether this is simply a manifestation of a cruel and punishing superego or an almighty omnipresent being—how do you test that out?

Perhaps behavioural experiments? Intentionally thinking about impure thoughts during Sunday prayers? Reading the bible backwards and writing a letter to Saint Teresa in the style of Christopher Hitchens?

The tricky bit is that the outcome of the experiment is so far off in the future. At the age of twenty-seven, you potentially have sixty-plus years before you find out whether you are sitting at the pearly gates or you're en route to the ninth circle of Hell.

In cases of religious scrupulosity, it can sometimes be helpful to steer clients toward their local, trusted faith leaders. Sometimes, there is sufficient softening of the hold the obsessions have over the person. ERP may then feel more doable, and resilience to the intrusive thoughts builds over time. But in some cases, even supported awareness does little to relieve it.

Rather than confusion, people commonly report a sense of dissonance despite the absence of evidence, so we need to dig a bit deeper down.

Regardless of whether themes of OCD are religious or moral scrupulosity, sexually taboo thoughts and images, or death by contamination or disease, the endpoint almost always leads to some form of predicted rejection, loss, or isolation.

So we get curious. What's the bottom line?

Different therapists will use different approaches to understand this. My favoured way is to draw from the concept of *Schemas* by Dr Jeffrey Young.[21]

Not that I'm a "schema therapist" per se, but I find the conceptual framework very useful in coming to a tangible shared understanding with a client.

The term schema simply refers to an entrenched and repeated cognitive, emotional, behavioural, and relational pattern. I've outlined some of the most common I see in practice. Do keep in mind that there are many schemas, and they often differ from person to person; these are simply examples.

So, if you say or do something you perceive as sinful or immoral, what does that say about you?

"I am bad, guilty, a terrible human, offensive to mankind."

But then what?

What's the final thought at the bottom of all of that—what really bothers you the most?

Well—

"Everyone will hate me; I will be rejected."

Sure! And then what happens? What's the consequence?

"I will be isolated—alone [*insert destination of choice*]: in prison, hospital, psychiatric unit, purgatory, or bus shelter—unemployable because society finds me abhorrent for eating lettuce imported from Spain."

—Okay. So, imagine [*powerful being*] finds out you're a terrible human, and you're now heading for [*destination of choice*]; what does that say about you now?

"I'm ANXIOUS!"

Yes, you're starting to feel afraid, but what's the bottom line? If you turn that into an *"I AM"* statement, what does it say about you now?

"I am helpless? Worthless? Unlovable? Powerless?"

Here, is where we typically break ground.

Helpless

This is a common schema, particularly where people describe feelings of excessive responsibility. Often linked to the *dependence/incompetence* schema, people can struggle with decisions, avoid independence, or freeze when faced with too much responsibility or unfamiliar tasks. This can develop in childhood if caregivers are overprotective, overly critical, or fail to encourage autonomy and resilience.

Surrendering to the schema might look like constant reassurance-seeking (seeking help), but it doesn't settle the worry or fear (no one can help). *Overcompensation* may appear more rigid, highly controlled, and overly independent: lots of researching, self-monitoring, and working things out alone.

Powerless

This often aligns closely with the *vulnerability to harm or illness* and *subjugation* schemas. With vulnerability, the person lives in chronic fear of disasters, illness, or loss of control. In subjugation, they feel that their own needs, opinions, or desires must be suppressed to avoid punishment or abandonment. Both schemas leave the person feeling like they lack control over their life and are at the mercy of others or fate. Unpredictable childhood environments and controlling or fear-driven environments are often involved in the formation of the belief system.

Surrender might result in the person deferring entirely to external authority, fearing dire consequences. *Overcompensation* may involve trying to exert power over others, overcorrecting behaviour, or making numerous attempts to maintain control or safety.

Worthless

Typically, this is rooted in feelings of *defectiveness or shame*. People with traits of this schema tend to perceive themselves as inherently flawed. They expect rejection, criticism, or humiliation if their true self is revealed. This can manifest as chronic self-criticism, hiding parts of themselves, or sabotaging relationships to avoid the pain of eventual rejection. The belief often develops in response to childhood experiences of shaming, criticism, or conditional acceptance. I also see this commonly in adults who struggled at school, particularly in making friends or with academic work.

Surrender to the schema may manifest as passive guilt and self-loathing in response to intrusive thoughts, proving to themselves they are morally repugnant. *Overcompensation* may generate feelings of excessive self-sacrifice, going out of their way to be morally good or self-denying to prove worth and compensate for shame. It can also manifest as harsh internal judgment directed at others, serving as a means to shift attention away from their own perceived sense of defects.

Unlovable

In many cases, this sits firmly in the *emotional deprivation* and *abandonment* schemas. Emotional deprivation is the expectation that others will not provide emotional support, empathy, and care. Abandonment is the fear that those we depend on will leave or cannot be relied upon to stay. Both schemas feed the belief that someone is not worthy of lasting love or closeness. These patterns often arise in early relationships marked by emotional distance, loss, or inconsistent caregiving.

Surrender might involve feeling inherently unacceptable or *cut off* from love due to intrusive thoughts, believing that their presence in a community is undeserved. *Overcompensation* may appear as an excessive need to earn love or approval.

A lot of people relate to multiple schemas; they can often overlap and will stem from different and mixed experiences.

Regardless, one thing for certain is that pleasing all people at all times is literally impossible. Even people with similar beliefs and values will be nuanced.

I mean, yes, follow the law of the land. That's absolutely sensible, most likely to prevent you from ever being locked in an actual prison. Try to be kind to people. Again, hell yes, but try to adopt a bit of that for yourself, if and where you can.

But what's missing? What needs might be going unmet? That's likely to be different for each person, but spending a little time noticing that might at least help you know where to begin.

When anxiety is high, it may not always feel like you have a choice. But if you have a punishing politician that is renting space for free in your mind, telling it to piss off once in a while might create a bit of room to think. Provide some space for compassion and care. What would that be like?

On a final note, it's worth mentioning that I was banned from Sunday school when I was twelve. I put my feet in a bowl of water when the group leader told us the story of Jesus walking on the Sea of Galilee. I was a tenacious pre-teen. It was entirely premeditated and intentional to prove a point.

If, by any slim chance, you do end up in Dante's Hell, and you need a decent therapist—look me up!

I'll be on the sixth floor.

6

Echo's Chamber

We are the only creatures who can conceive of our own appearance, and are haunted by it

—Rollo May

We can all become absorbed with self-image at times.

Not in the malignant ways of Rader, Hindley, or Brady. More typical of normal modern life. Some people struggle to accept criticism and intentionally seek admiration and attention. It's common to want to be noticed. At times, you may hold the belief that you are better than others to manage feelings of inadequacy. However, if we were to trust everything sold to us online, we would be forgiven for thinking that anyone who shows off a bit, spends a lot of time on their appearance, or self-promotion must be "a narcissist".

Mostly, this is not the case.

Still, we currently live in a world where appearance matters, and it is often rewarded. How you present yourself can significantly impact your presence both socially and professionally. It can affect your chances of success and even influence how easily you're accepted by others.

In the UK, the market for cosmetic procedures has more than doubled in the past decade.[1] The cosmetic industry isn't entirely responsible for appearance insecurity, but arguably, it has certainly monetised it. Whether you are spending three-figure sums for the latest hairdo or non-surgical procedures such as Botox, dermal fillers, and thread lifts, physical self-improvement has become increasingly popular. You can even order a set of new teeth online these days.

Yet, while many people pursue self-enhancement with clear intent and autonomy, the line between improvement and emotional management isn't always so clear. Of course, putting a lot of your energy into your appearance does not mean that you have a mental health problem. It doesn't necessarily mean you are a narcissist, either.

The original story behind the label carries more depth than most modern discussions tend to suggest.

For anyone who hasn't come across the myth of Narcissus before, there are many variations of it. Mostly, it is interpreted as a story of egocentric vanity and is strongly associated with clinical terms such as narcissistic personality disorder (NPD). However, there are also dynamics within the story that, from my perspective, are highly relevant to obsession and compulsion. Particularly those between Narcissus and Echo.

Who doesn't like a bit of morbid Greek tragedy over technical diagrams and arrows? What follows is loosely based on Ovid's version, *Metamorphoses*. Apologies in advance to anyone who is an expert in classical mythology.

* ✳ *

Narcissus is a beautiful young man who has many admirers. Still, he hasn't shown any particular interest in anyone, being somewhat aloof and emotionally detached. This is starting to annoy the gods and it's testing their patience.

Meanwhile, Echo, a mountain nymph who is a keen chatterbox, has been keeping the god Hera talking while Zeus has been *visiting* other nymphs, and she's covering up for him. Hera is absolutely livid, and curses Echo, taking her freedom to ever speak freely again. Now, she is compelled only to repeat the last words that other people say to her.

One day, Echo spots Narcissus. Obviously, he's a very handsome young chap and she immediately falls in love with him. She starts following him around silently, watching him from a distance without him knowing.

—She's technically a stalker, but let's run with it.

Because Echo has been cursed she is unable to speak first, so she just waits, hiding in the background.

Narcissus suddenly gets the sense that he's possibly being watched. So he calls out. "Is anyone here?" Echo replies. "Here!"

Eventually, she steps out into view and tries to embrace Narcissus. He immediately rejects her. She can only repeat his last word. "Away!" Devastated, Echo retreats to the mountains and stays there until she fades away. Only her voice remains.

Narcissus continues to reject potential suitors, and one of them gets very upset and prays to the gods. Nemesis, the god of retribution, decides to curse Narcissus to fall in love with his own reflection. A while later, Narcissus is hunting in the forest; it's thirsty work, and he kneels down to drink from a still pond. He becomes captivated by his own image.

"Who is this marvellous young person?"

The catch is that he doesn't realise it's his own reflection. He starts to reach out and connect to the young man in the pond, trying to touch and kiss him—his own image. Each time he tries to connect, the water is disturbed, and the image distorts or vanishes. So he stays very still, trying to preserve it, and is unable to pull himself away.

Eventually, he begins to realise that no matter how hard he tries to connect to the image in the pool, the object he desires can never love him back. Narcissus eventually withers away by the side of the pond and dies. Alone.

The distant voice of Echo can only repeat his final word. "Farewell."

A flower grows in the place where Narcissus lay.

Both are lost.

Cheery old story.

While there are definitely elements around vanity, it's also a cautionary tale to warn against the kind of hyper-focus that can keep people separated from true connection, both with others and themselves. Narcissus is trapped in a cycle of false images and beliefs. Echo is left repeating the words of others, having no voice of her own. Together, the emotional cost is isolation, self-alienation, and one-sided longings where no actual dialogue or intimacy can exist.

In many cases, people who experience obsessive-compulsive problems can become very fixated on things. But rather than an inflated and grandiose sense of self, it's commonly an exaggerated sense of personal defectiveness. The person's sense of agency and autonomy becomes muted, complying with an internal critic, compelled only to repeat back its words.

Don't get me wrong, many of us look in the mirror and dislike aspects of our appearance. If I look at my own reflection, I'm under no illusion that the image of a middle-aged bloke with droopy eyelids, wrinkles and grey hair is my own. But having spent my early years worrying that I would be dead before I reached my twenties, part of me is grateful for those lines on my face. That doesn't mean that I have to like the look of them.

But for some people, what they see in the mirror extends beyond perfectionism and also what is objectively realistic.

Imagine what life would be like if every time you saw your own reflection, the image looking back at you was consistently distorted. All you can see are subjective physical faults and flaws that other people can't see. No matter how much you touch them or try to keep them still, the more exaggerated the flaws, and the more defective the areas of concern appear.

However, a psychologist's office is one of the least likely places that someone might initially present when they experience these types of difficulties.

Simone has been a beauty therapist for over fifteen years, recently opening a hair and beauty salon in a swanky part of town. Simone and her business partner Charles, a hairdresser, have been friends since college, and neither has ever worked in a mental health setting.

Given the nature of their industry, they are both aware that some of their clients likely come into the salon with problems that have a psychological basis. But they've never used terms like *trichotillomania*, or *dermatillomania*.

They just know that some of their clients mechanically pull out their own hair, often from the scalp, eyebrows and eyelashes. This sometimes causes bald patches. Other people pick at their skin, sometimes around imperfections, which can cause sore patches and wounds that may lead to permanent scarring. Both conditions can cause distress.

Charles usually talks to his clients about practical ways to reduce stress, as well as alternative actions to try to interrupt the cycle. In some cases, the bald patches can be visually disguised or improved with clever cutting techniques. For people who don't realise they are doing it, Charles has some fancy products that contain minoxidil to promote hair growth, leaving a residue and changing the tactile sensation.

With skin issues, Simone will work with her clients to help them establish new skincare routines that promote healing and reduce scarring and will sometimes refer them to a dermatologist where necessary.

But some of their clients leave them both feeling perplexed and frustrated, which leads them to overly personalise things.

It's 8.30 am and Simone and Charles are going through their diaries before their first clients arrive.

[Simone] (sighing) Oh fffff—fffuuck's sake!

[Charles] What's wrong with you now?

[Simone] You've got Natalia at 9 am. I'm going to work downstairs. DO NOT, and I MEAN—DO NOT tell her I'm free to come up to speak to her.

[Charles] (laughing) I don't know why you hate her so much. She's sassy, but I like her!

[Simone] I don't hate her; she just makes me anxious. I can't do anything right for her.

[Charles] Well—she keeps booking in with you.

[Simone] She does, but it's every other bloody week, Charles. It's like she's got that OCD or something. I'm scared to do anything. She's had lip filler corrections four times now, saying that her mouth still looks wonky since the first time I did it.

[Charles] Not everyone has my eye for detail, darling. We can't all be perfect.

[Simone] And modest, Charles, you forget your modesty. Seriously, though, there's nothing wrong with the filler. She was asking about Botox last time.

[Charles] Botox? Isn't she like nineteen or something?

[Simone] Exactly. Her skin is really good.

[Charles] Maybe she just wants it to be perfectly flawless like mine (preening in the mirror).

[Simone] You're not helping me here, Charles.

[Charles] QUEEEEN! Go fly off to your bat cave and leave her to me. I'll sort it out.

Natalia is an aspiring model trying to break into the fashion industry. She's very friendly and often talks to Charles about their shared passion for clothing design. However, Natalia always avoids looking at herself in the mirror, which Charles puts down to her being shy and not liking eye contact.

She also spends ages pulling her hair onto her face before she leaves the salon. Charles is meticulous, and it annoys him when she does it, leaving him feeling that he hasn't styled her hair how she wanted it.

Today, Charles has been dealing with a booking while Natalia has been getting her hair washed by his assistant. She's looking in the mirror, touching her face. When Charles walks over, her face is flushed red, and she is on the edge of tears.

[Charles] Is everything okay? You seem upset.

[Natalia] Sort of (now tearful).

[Charles] Tell me what's upsetting you.

[Natalia] Would it be possible to speak to Simone?

[Charles] She's back to back all morning. Can I help?

[Natalia] Not really, I want to ask her about Botox.

[Charles] Yeah—so, Simone did mention you had spoken to her about that. What's going on?

[Natalia] This side of my mouth always looks lower than the other (pointing it out).

[Charles] QUEEEEN!—STOP!—IT! Your face is fabulous! Like you just stepped off the front cover of *Vogue*. Don't worry about it.

Natalia instantly feels ashamed, and her face and neck flush red, again. She is clearly struggling to hold back her tears.

Charles isn't sure what's going on, but he feels bad. His theatrical praise normally makes his regular clients feel good about themselves. He didn't mean to upset her, and apologises.

Over the remaining appointment time, Natalia explains to Charles that she has had long-standing concerns with her nose and mouth looking asymmetrical. She thinks this is holding her back from being selected for higher-profile jobs with the modelling agency. Natalia has been working two bar jobs and staying on a friend's sofa to save up for surgery.

Charles tells Natalia that he thinks she is "crazy" for thinking that way, and he can't for the life of him see what she is talking about. "Some of my other clients would kill for a face like yours. You really need to start speaking to yourself better!" Natalia's face flushes crimson, and she tries to change the subject.

At the end of the appointment, Natalia quickly gets out of her seat and pays for the service. She leaves the salon feeling too embarrassed to go back to see Charles again.

For people who experience the clinical signs and symptoms of body dysmorphic disorder (BDD), there is a pervasive and intense preoccupation with perceived defects in their physical body. This can include appearance concerns that cause significant distress. Usually, the faults and flaws are either not observable to others or are objectively seen as very slight imperfections compared to how the person views them.

As with other types of obsessive-compulsive problems, there is a cycle between thoughts, emotions and actions that maintains it. Some people spend a lot of time checking in the mirror, and others avoid mirrors altogether. There can also be compulsive grooming rituals, a tendency to seek reassurance about perceived faults, or a constant comparison to others. Sometimes, these are mental compulsions carried out inside the person's mind, such as visualising or mentally altering their appearance.

This can often lead to people being misunderstood and perceived as vain, awkward, or fussy. Attempts to overly reassure someone that their faults and flaws either do not exist or are not noticeable can be perceived as minimising and shaming. It's not necessarily the case that it is being done with bad intentions, but it can leave the person feeling less willing to speak up or seek help. This can also happen in healthcare settings. The signs of BDD are sometimes missed, or seen as a minor issue.[2]

While there is often an objective difference between how the person sees themselves compared to what other people notice, the belief can be held with such conviction that insight into what the person can subjectively see versus what is more objectively true can be entirely absent.[3]

In a lot of cases, people won't seek psychological support at all. Instead, they experience it as a physical problem and seek out cosmetic procedures. This often results in unsatisfactory outcomes or failure to resolve the issue. It can also generate further scrutiny around new areas of dissatisfaction and, in turn, fuel the desire to seek out further procedures.[4]

The intrusive nature of the cycle does overlap to some degree with more classical OCD. However, BDD is seen as a separate condition, and the focus of the obsessions and compulsions are usually highly specific to facial features, hair, skin imperfections, or perceived anatomical defects.

Sometimes, there is a more intensive focus on the person's body shape, particularly in specific areas relating to body mass. In these cases, there can also be a degree of overlap with the features typically seen with conditions such as anorexia nervosa or bulimia.[5]

The clinical signs and symptoms of BDD are typically reported more in females, but it's becoming increasingly common in men. This includes sensitivities ranging from hairline recession to muscle mass. Sometimes, people may undergo surgical procedures, such as liposuction, to achieve a perfectly flat waistline and defined abs despite maintaining high levels of physical fitness.

Medical professionals have described cases where their patients have undergone multiple surgeries, such as rhinoplasties or jaw realignments, despite objectively proportionate features and no medical indication for correction.[6][7] In these cases, surgery hasn't been pursued to improve appearance in the conventional sense but to eliminate the perceived flaws.[8][9]

Similar to OCD and perfectionism, body-focused concerns commonly begin during adolescence. Self-consciousness is often heightened around this time, particularly relating to our developing bodies and our emerging sense of physical attraction and sexuality.

Varied factors may contribute to someone being more at risk of developing BDD, such as trauma, upbringing, and personality traits. However, these also need to be contextualised within wider social and cultural messages.

———— * ✳ * ————

It would be comforting to think that body image is a purely personal matter shaped only by the unique ways that our brains overestimate or exaggerate. But our beliefs about appearance and the comparisons we commonly make are also shaped through our social lives, history, and culture.

We absorb language, images, and commercial advertising. Early family scripts can also have an influence. "Don't eat that; you'll get fat and no one will like you." Throughout our school years, we tend to copy trends and fashions, watching popular kids from the sidelines. Trying to emulate, learning to equate image with status and popularity.

However, the social messages around body image and appearance have never been neutral. Bodies have been scrutinised, classified, and assigned meaning for millennia.

In early Western medicine, the shape of our bodies and facial features were actually believed to reveal things about our personality or character. A crooked nose or an asymmetrical face would imply that we were morally corrupt or of poor intelligence. Which is entirely nonsense, of course. Still, these types of assumptions subtly influenced everything from criminal profiling to early psychiatric diagnosis.

In 19th-century Europe, colonial powers used similar ideas to construct hierarchies of race. Physical features were catalogued and ranked: skin tone, nose shape, and hair texture. White European bodies were idealised as the default benchmark.[10]

Throughout modern history, visible disabilities or differences have been consistently stigmatised. The ideal body is defined not just by its symmetry or thinness but also by its ability to function and be productive. People with chronic illness, disfigurement, or non-normative movement were treated as problems to be fixed, managed, or hidden.[11] The legacy of this is still visible today.

After World War II, being thin became a dominant ideal in the West. Initially, it was associated with affluence and self-control. To be slim wasn't simply about attractiveness; it was symbolic of someone disciplined and self-restrained. People with fuller bodies became medicalised, treated not only as a health risk but as a failure of moral character, lacking control.

Naturally, we are an imperfect species. Our bodies come in different shapes and sizes, our skin tones vary, and we are all susceptible to the ageing process, which includes sagging and wrinkling. We are vulnerable to disease, injury, and deterioration. This is what makes us beautifully human.

However, the 24/7 relentless social messages in the background can make psychological treatment difficult, particularly for someone with body-focused concerns Realistically, those messages are unlikely to cease anytime soon.

---

* ✳ *

Navigating all of this can become quite complicated when someone actually enters therapy. It can often feel as though you are working upstream, particularly with the prominence of social media in people's lives these days.

With CBT-based approaches, the focus is often on helping the person modify their belief system. As you might imagine, trying to help someone disconfirm the belief "I am fat and ugly" is unstable ground to work on.

While beauty is always in the eye of the beholder, many people find themselves falling short of narrow, conventional ideals. This can make it very difficult to challenge appearance-related beliefs using standard strategies, especially in the face of feedback from the social world. In some cases, these beliefs are deeply ingrained and consistently reinforced through exposure to media, peers, and systems.

Clients can often experience ambivalence toward the therapeutic change process, especially when their frame of reference is rooted in a realistic social context.[12] This is where the importance of relationships is absolutely key.

For example, a psychodynamic therapist might think about BDD in terms of early emotional struggles in the person's closest and most intimate relationships. A way of managing deeper-rooted, unbearable feelings around a sense of defectiveness linked to their personal worth.[13]

The focus on physical flaws is more about the anxiety of being unlovable or rejected. From this perspective, the aim of therapy might be to explore the implicit meanings of what the symptoms represent and support the person in developing a stronger and more stable sense of themselves.

Humanistic approaches, such as person-centred therapy, might consider body-focused issues in terms of Carl Rogers' idea of incongruence.[14] In this framework, BDD may be seen through the lens of early environmental messages. How someone may have come to learn that the only way they can be worthy of love or acceptance is to present a perfect version of themselves. Perhaps the person grew up feeling that they only had worth or value when they looked a particular way or met certain conditions.

With any therapeutic model, a central theme in helping someone with BDD is basically trying to help the person loosen the bind between their appearance and self-devaluing. Whether this is through cognitive restructuring, emotional exploration, or relational repair. It's not necessarily how someone looks that's the core issue, but what their appearance means about them.

A fundamental part of helping someone regain a sense of control over their difficulties is understanding the difference between self-worth and self-esteem. While they are similar, there is an important distinction between them.

Self-worth is our sense of value in the world. Our feeling of being loved, of mattering to someone. Being important just as we are. "I am only lovable if I achieve this standard." Self-esteem, on the other hand, tends to relate more to comparison, achievement, competence, and capability. "If I can't do my job perfectly, I'm a terrible employee."

Some people struggle with both.

Either way, people with internally demanding standards can spend a lot of excess energy berating themselves in the pursuit of betterment. Whether this is aesthetic, career, or material gains. Inevitably, it always catches up. At some point, the body will freeze, shut down, or burn out. In some cases, depressive symptoms start to show up. This can include prolonged periods of fatigue, loss of interest in things, or a lack of motivation to get out of bed in the morning. This can also involve thoughts of not wanting to exist anymore.

What is particularly concerning is that those who don't seek help often present with higher risks. There is a strong correlation between BDD and increased suicidal ideation. Around a quarter of people have attempted suicide, and two-thirds report a history of suicidal thoughts.[15]

The statistics are pretty alarming. Many people spend years battling a self-image that others cannot see, often without appropriate support. Naturally, there may be a tendency to withdraw and self-isolate, trying to avoid life altogether out of fear of embarrassment or shame.

But trying to constantly control how the world perceives you, by curating a more idealised, more acceptable self, becomes exhausting. Somewhere along the way, people become lost.

With any problem, if we spend too much time getting excessively tangled up in issues of worth or esteem, it becomes hard to tell the difference between our own voice and the echo of the world around us. We end up stuck in our own heads, trying to perfect the image, listening to the reverb.

And it rarely does what we want it to.

If you stood in a room full of people, it's unlikely everyone would see you the same way. Some would be impressed. Some would be indifferent. Some wouldn't like you at all, and not always for reasons that make sense. That's realistic of life.

You could have the face of Narcissus, and still be met with envy, criticism, or disinterest. You cannot control what other people see, or how they think.

So what's the point?

If you enjoy putting effort into your appearance, or it gives you confidence, then fair enough. Go with that! There's no shame in wanting to feel good in your own skin. But if it's mostly about shielding yourself from judgment, then it's a lot of work for not much payoff.

Might you be getting in your own way?

Wouldn't it be better to show up as you are, not as who you imagine others want you to be?

And it isn't just body image where comparison seeps in. Many of us spend tremendous amounts of energy trying to stay one step ahead, fixating on thoughts, micromanaging details, trying to avoid mistakes or *correcting* ourselves after the fact.

For some, it isn't cosmetic procedures they reach for. Rather, job titles, promotions, and income brackets. Laser-focusing on success in the fragile hope that, eventually, it will silence the echo of doubt.

—Heads up. Typically, it doesn't.

Not for long, anyway.

7
Avoiding Cracks

The greatest hazard of all, losing one's self
— Søren Kierkegaard

Tim's house was a grand-looking property on a hill.

He was my fourth therapist, and while not the last, it was by far the longest I've been in treatment. By this point, I was a practising clinician but still in training, and I wanted to experience psychodynamic therapy first-hand. There would be a three-hour round trip from home each week to meet in person, which wasn't high up the convenience list, but finding an affordable therapist with availability around my schedule was worth it. I would arrive early each week, parking away from the house, and then spend ten minutes inspecting the soles of my shoes for mud and dog faeces.

Logically, there was nothing on them, having just got out of the car. But on the off chance of potentially being banished from Tim's pristine hallway due to unknowingly trailing an unpleasant substance, I kept checking.

Tim had asked me to arrive on time but not early. He had a patient before me, and there was no receptionist, so I would hang out on a side street before the appointment.

13:58: I walked to the house, carefully watching my step on the pavement and closing the gate firmly, pushing and pulling it. I would occasionally hear a little dog barking and had intrusive thoughts of it being crushed by a car. It would be my fault for not closing the gate properly.

13:59: Eight steps further, a final quick check of my shoes, and then wait.

14:00: I pressed the bell. Tim would promptly open the door to greet his most impressive patient. Arriving precisely as instructed, paying promptly when requested, and caring enough about a dog I'd never met that the gate was coming loose. I also never missed or cancelled a session.

Tim reminded me of one of my old high school music teachers. A kind man but difficult to read. I learned early on that treating *therapy for therapists* as an extended supervision exercise simply kept my true feelings at a distance. That still didn't stop me from doing it.

In fact, I was more bothered about admitting to Tim that I was entirely clueless about what we were doing than talking about my problems. I wanted to work everything out in advance before I could trust the process. Being very familiar with structured therapy such as CBT, I didn't really want that. But the novelty of *free association* and *sitting with not knowing* wore off pretty quickly. I began feeling increasingly lost over the first six months.

I checked into therapy partly due to training requirements and mostly because I wanted to get to the root of my illogical obsession with disease and terminal illness. Instead, I would mostly talk about work and the stress of training, and I always found a way to mention impressive achievements.

Each offering would be met with a simple nod and an unimpressed gaze. We would often sit in silence, sometimes looking out of the window. It was rarely predictable when he spoke. Sometimes, Tim would go for a monologue; other times, just the one word across the whole session.

While CBT still retains its title as the most empirically supported treatment of OCD, from my perspective, dynamic psychotherapy is better suited when it comes to personality-led difficulties. The primary reason for this is that there is a greater emphasis on the early years of development, during which more ingrained patterns have typically formed.

In psychodynamic theory, obsessive-compulsive symptoms and perfectionistic traits are not necessarily viewed in the same way as more structured treatments. Without any significant depth of training in the concepts, they can be difficult to understand and are often caricatured.

Sometimes, they are taken literally rather than as metaphorical principles for thinking about the development of human relationships. There are many different schools of thought, but with a single unifying concept.

The human experience of love and loss.

Granted, that may sound less exotic than stories about sexual desire for a parent or penis envy, but love is our capacity to bond and form intimate relationships with others. This includes the quality, safety and nurture within those relationships. Loss is our capacity to tolerate being separated from, as well as losing significant others, including the inevitable endings and death experienced in the reality of life.

One of the central ideas surrounding obsession and compulsion is that the symptoms emerge from a conflict between our internal drives (*the id*) and a harsh, internalised critic who demands compliance and is hell-bent on morality and authority (*the superego*).[1]

The drives themselves may not be anything out of the ordinary, such as resentment, sexual curiosity, competitiveness, or a longing for attention and care. Yet, the critical superego perceives these as dangerous, morally unacceptable, or shameful.

The psychoanalyst Betty Joseph argued that obsessional thinking and compulsive behaviour function as defences against emotional intimacy.[2] Rather than directly experiencing sadness, anger, guilt, envy, or shame, we instead become absorbed in repetitive thoughts and actions. It creates a false sense of control, but the emotional conflicts remain unresolved.

Because these internal pressures are often unconscious, *the ego* (our moderating referee) can't cope, and this gives rise to intense feelings of anxiety. This leaves the person feeling both lost and stuck on repeat.

There is also a lot of emphasis on "defences". These are a bit more complex than "safety behaviours" in CBT, but are essentially the ways we have learned to manage strong feelings in childhood. They become emotional management strategies that we continue to adopt in our adult lives.

For example, perfectionism might reflect the defences of *reaction formation* or *undoing*. Where the person unconsciously transforms an unacceptable feeling into its opposite. Someone who feels intense envy might show excessive admiration or generosity towards the same person. Someone who experiences aggressive or hostile impulses may instead present as polite, accommodating, or excessively conscientious.

Undoing, may involve attempts to symbolically cancel out their unacceptable feelings through ritualised behaviours or being overly responsible or morally rigid. Trying to get rid of the emotion or impulse.[3]

Another defence is the *isolation of affect*, where the emotion being generated is disconnected from the person's thoughts.[4] For example, when someone can talk about issues or challenges that would typically generate a substantial rise of emotion, they can describe them in a flat, emotionless tone, as if telling you about what happened in the latest episode of their favourite soap opera. The thought and emotions become *split off*.

People with deeply entrenched patterns of emotional avoidance can struggle with exposure. If the pressure to confront their fear is too high, it can either lead to complete disengagement or detachment from emotions during sessions, which is typically unproductive.[5]

* ✳ *

Naturally, strong emotions can feel unpleasant, even frightening, but they carry useful information.

Guilt is commonly encountered in therapy and often described as disproportionate. But it's frequently confused with shame. Often, this stems from thoughts and fears fuelled by blame. This can create intense emotional distress, particularly when someone perceives a failure to meet a moral, social, or ethical standard.

Commonly, the content of intrusive thoughts in OCD can also bring up complex emotions. In turn, this can generate a significant amount of anxiety. This is the physiological threat response in the body, not necessarily the emotion of fear. Obviously, fear is often in the mix. But more often than not, so is anger, guilt and shame.

In my opinion, understanding the difference between guilt and shame is important when considering long-term problems with obsession and compulsion. Particularly, where there has been limited response to prior attempts at psychological intervention such as ERP.

Although it can feel highly unpleasant, guilt is fundamental to human existence and social cohesion. It supports our capacity for remorse and our impulse to resolve and repair relationships. It is typically physically felt in the body as tightness or pressure in the throat and heaviness in the chest. Our body posture can appear more withdrawn. The feelings often come in waves, linked to thoughts around remorse or a wish to make amends.[6]

Shame, on the other hand, is an entirely different entity. It is often felt in response to criticism and blame, driving the impulse to avoid, undo, withdraw, or push away. Shame is usually experienced in the body as a sinking hollow feeling deep in the pit of the stomach, often combined with flushing of the face and neck. This is a common symptom with people who experience social anxiety and phobias.[7]

It makes sense when we consider that the underlying schema at play with socially based fear is often the self-perception of the person being shameful or defective compared to the broader social world.[8]

However, guilt is a more productive emotion, encouraging us to acknowledge a mistake and take responsibility. Shame tends to be paralysing. It leads to self-judgement rather than accountability, self-criticism rather than compassion, and a repeating pattern of avoidance and self-punishment.[9]

Shame and blame tend to be closely linked when it comes to obsession and compulsion, but they are fundamentally different. Shame is an emotion, and blame is an action. Shame is something we *feel* in response to a stimulus; blame is something we *do* in response to the feeling.

When faced with feelings of shame, it is common for someone, particularly with an early history of blaming, to unconsciously shift the assignment of responsibility, whether inward—"I am bad—others are good." Or, outward—"I am good—others are bad."

While blame can sometimes appear in the context of acknowledging viable personal fault, such as jumping a red light and causing a car crash, it is also a common defence mechanism that serves to avoid emotional discomfort.

Again, it's not just the intrusive thoughts that trigger anxiety, but the fear that they point to something blameworthy. A constant dread of being falsely accused, held responsible, criticised, or exposed. Not just being seen as faulty in themselves, but also being held accountable for these faults. Often, predicting dire social consequences.

The common thread is a pervasive pattern of blaming and an ongoing fear of being judged or found out, regardless of how minor the perceived offence.

The problem with this, is that it can also lead to the avoidance of more realistic responsibilities. A person might spend three hours consumed with dashcam footage, fearing they hit a pedestrian on the way home. Yet, feel less urgency to engage in meaningful activities that align with their values, such as spending time with their kids.

Instead of allowing for the natural discomfort of unwarranted guilt, the compulsive viewing of the dashcam functions to avoid the potential risk of being blamed. Then, going to prison and being separated from the kids. Realistically, it just keeps them locked up in a repetitive cycle that offers no real resolution and still distances them from their kids.

A zero-sum game.

The key distinction is that guilt, based on objective wrongdoing, can guide a person towards positive change. Shame inevitably leads to stagnation.

When people view themselves as inherently bad rather than acknowledging a mistake or imperfection, they become stuck in automatic self-punishment rather than embracing their choice to engage with repair. In many cases, the relationship most in need of urgent repair is the one with themselves.

Essentially, psychodynamic therapy isn't about trying to turn your life into a Greek tragedy. It's more concerned with what's realistic about being human.

The primary aim is to help people understand how they manage their experiences. Assisting the person to be more in touch with objective reality and address problematic patterns that may be getting in the way of living their life more fully.

＊ ✳ ＊

On the narrow winding lanes, about fifteen minutes from Tim's house, the traffic reached a standstill due to a fatal collision.

While I would normally have time to spare, I had to cancel my appointment. The following week, I decided to tell Tim that I felt very angry while stuck in traffic and had to miss the session. I thought this would be of interest to him, as I rarely spoke about emotions.

At the time, I could just see a line of traffic and was consumed with anxiety about having a "late cancellation" on my meticulous record. I was blaming road works and lack of traffic updates. I didn't know there had been a fatality until I saw the news later that evening. But I was worried that Tim might think I was psychopathic. That isn't a desirable trait in a professional psychologist, so I embellished the story with other emotions, such as sadness, guilt, and grief.

I spent ten minutes anxiously tying myself in rambling knots, explaining the fundamental experience of being stuck in traffic and how this might link to Tim. Admittedly, I was also trying to impress him, showing off a bit, making rehearsed links to the principles of attachment theory that I'd read the night before. Tim glanced out of the window, then directly back at me.

"It's like you're trying to bite the breast."

—Silence.

Truth be told, I didn't have a clue what he meant at the time, but from the reading I was doing, I knew it was likely therapy speak for my dysfunctional attachments being played out with him. I had clearly revealed too much and was now caught in his headlights. I lost control of the narrative.

Now, internally scrambling against bizarre intrusive thoughts of being breastfed by Tim while suppressing the childish fit of giggles going off like a bomb inside me. My stomach rumbled loudly due to anxiety and having skipped lunch before setting off.

My options: Clarify what he said? Laugh? Definitely not. So I focused on the knots in my stomach, tried to look thoughtful, and kept glancing at the clock—14:48, it was nearly over.

A Google search back at the car confirmed that Tim was a fan of Melanie Klein, an early psychoanalyst famous for her seminal work observing children. He was referring to frustration in the attachment, longing for care while resenting its absence.

Regardless, I spent the long drive home flitting between two positions. On the one hand, anxious that Tim perceived me as puerile and not taking therapy seriously. On the other hand, it all sounded somewhat of a stretch and I considered sacking him off as my therapist.

Melanie Klein developed the idea that the experience of our internal emotional world is shaped in relation to how we experience others, forming what she called *internal objects*.

Naturally, during very early life, a baby is entirely dependent on its caregivers for survival. According to Klein, the representation of the mother's breast isn't simply a source of food and nourishment but also symbolic of nurture, safety, frustration, and loss.[10]

As infants, we can't yet experience our caregiver as a whole person, so they become *split* into parts. A "good" part that feeds, soothes, and comforts. A "bad" part that is sometimes absent, late with food, or unsatisfying.

When the baby is overwhelmed by hunger, discomfort, or distress, they may succumb to *murderous rage*, an infant *"phantasy"* of attacking or devouring the breast. The source of its anger, rage, abandonment, and disappointment.

Again, it's important to understand these are conceptual frameworks not literal accounts of what babies think, feel, or remember. It is more of a provocative image depicting how "aggressive fantasies" represent the beginnings of our early inner emotional conflicts.

For example, if you attack your object of love, care, or safety, what happens if they then disappear for good?

Klein saw our early experiences as foundational in developing healthy feelings and impulses. In her view, normative development involves a shift from the *paranoid-schizoid position*, where the infant splits objects into all-good or all-bad parts, to the *depressive position*, where the child begins to integrate these parts and perceive others as whole, ambiguous objects. Capable of being both loved and hated, good and bad. [11]

Although these ideas originated from observing infant development, they are more commonly used in therapy settings to explore the dynamics playing out in adult experiences. Based on Klein's theory, where typical development is interrupted, or there are experiences of trauma in the attachment, integration can stall. The split parts become internalised and influence an emotional blueprint that is carried into adulthood.

For example, when emotions feel too intense or intimacy in relationships feels threatening, adults may still have a tendency to categorise people or things into more concrete extremes: good or bad, acceptable or unacceptable, right or wrong, safe or dangerous, clean or contaminated. An angel or a demon.

While I'm not necessarily evangelical about the theories and am quite pragmatic as a clinician, idealising and devaluing, or *"splitting,"* is definitely an emotional management strategy that I frequently encounter in my clinical practice. In most cases, it typically appears early in the therapeutic relationship.

Having sat on the opposite side of the therapy room for quite some time now, I have observed similar patterns to those occurring with Tim. Careful presentation, explicit efforts to impress, and the very guarded ways in which people will minimise or dismiss their struggles. They will avoid putting themselves in a vulnerable position that leaves them potentially open to criticism or perceived failure. Many people are seeking an alternative to CBT, but then scramble for an instruction manual after session three.

"Fascinating, James. So, how do I get rid of this feeling?!"

There are also common signs of emotional distancing and pressure for efficiency from the outset. Clients often do not realise, at least when referring to a therapist with a psychoanalytic lens, that the initial engagement process at the start of therapy is usually quite telling of their interpersonal process. Obviously, this is broadly applicable, not exclusive to compulsive-obsessive people. It's also a rough indication of the person rather than a specific measure or test.

But when you've read a lot of referrals and seen a significant number of patients, it's generally a good indicator of the likely barriers and blocks to therapy once someone begins. Quite often, there is an underlying sense of pressure to be self-sufficient, with little or no time for therapy. They want to do it well, just as quickly as possible, and preferably from an emotional distance.

Particularly with people who have perfectionistic tendencies, there are often rigidly high standards in play. Some people naturally find it difficult when others do not meet those standards. This generally goes one of two ways. On the one hand, denying faults and idealising—"An amazing therapist!" On the other hand, carefully monitoring for signs of incompetence, inconsistencies, and gaps in knowledge.

"A terrible therapist."

There is commonly a pull to become the "perfect therapist". This needs to be carefully monitored, especially if you're a therapist with similar tendencies. Equally, it can be challenging to resist the urge to overly praise and acknowledge the efforts that some patients will make.

However, this isn't simply a case of trying to bring someone down a peg or two. Commonly, the person will perceive a fragile and superficial quality to the relationship.

"You wouldn't like me if you really knew me."

"Look at this impressive thing over here instead."

These are usually tactical defences to distract and redirect, avoiding any depth of feeling toward the therapist and keeping them at arm's length.

Naturally, when the interpersonal stakes feel high, people tend to avoid any potential cracks that may reveal flaws and faults. In particular, any that may reveal more deeply held undesirable feelings and emotions such as guilt, shame, envy, and disgust. Behaviourally, this can take varied forms but commonly includes prompt arrival and attendance.

In private practice, invoices are paid within hours of receipt. Some clients will engage in extensive reading between sessions and attempt to engage the therapist in intellectual and theoretical discussions. Keeping their emotions watertight and the perception of the therapist as being interested and favourable. "Who *is* this marvellous and very clever person?"

At times, the opposite can happen, depending on the person's process. Although less common with perfectionists, clients will treat therapy with the same disregard and low value that they place on themselves; inconsistent attendance, late payment, constant complaining, or redirecting their main issues onto superficial problems and rants.

Either way, as a therapist, it can be hard not to get drawn into *splitting* ourselves into good or bad therapists. Also, resisting the view of our clients as good or bad patients.

Objectively, neither exists in reality.

Splitting can sometimes be marked and extreme, and when coupled with other problems, such as a very poor sense of self, regular turbulence in relationships, and rapid shifts in mood and anxiety, it can indicate more severe personality-based difficulties such as a borderline pattern.[12]

However, this isn't to say that splitting is inherently pathological; many people engage in some form of it, especially when they are under pressure or stress. Sometimes, people consistently opt for outward devaluing: constant criticism and contempt for others, avoiding feelings such as envy.[13] And sometimes there's not much room in between.

I use the metaphor *The Shelf of Marvellous Things* to describe this with patients. Tim would typically have a spot on the top shelf, rarely hitting the bin—though he came close once or twice. As humans, we more realistically sit somewhere in the messy middle. We're just not always comfortable with it.

People with obsessive-compulsive and perfectionistic traits tend to be particularly prone to struggling with this. Often, finding it difficult to straddle ambiguity, things being realistically average: both good and bad, admirable and flawed, competent and imperfect.

MARVELLOUS THINGS

USELESS THINGS

The Shelf of Marvellous Things

Therapists are not immune to these types of problems either. In the UK, perfectionism and high personal standards are particularly prevalent among trainee and aspiring practitioner psychologists. That's not to imply that everyone meets a clinical threshold, but the path to professional training is steep, requiring significant commitment to years of academic study.

There is also a highly selective intake process and intense competition for limited places. It stands to reason that the field attracts people with a demanding internal process.

But it's also equally common to get caught up in idealising within the profession itself. Sometimes, we tend to idealise certain types of therapists and their modalities while devaluing others. There's also some research to suggest that these types of traits may also make it harder for us, particularly trainees, to seek help if they start experiencing emotional difficulties.[14]

As much as it can sometimes be difficult for us to acknowledge, similar to our patients, these are our younger parts at play, often multiple parts. This isn't to say that we are all simply acting like children. Just the old pattern, some of the time, and in an adult form, mixed with healthier parts.

Take the experience I described when I was sitting in traffic. As an adult clinician, a healthy part of me could sit through endless sessions with Tim. Yet, my superego (commander in chief) is in the driving seat. Keeping things at an intellectual level so the cracks stay superglued together. But it was getting in the way of Tim knowing me.

Was I having an epic meltdown like a distressed toddler when I got stuck in traffic? Yes. Did a self-sufficient older part respond, turning the unrelenting demands inward and self-blaming? Yes. Then externalising blame to get rid of the guilt? Of course!

Was my internal response to Tim's question about the breast that of a healthy adult part? No!

It was that of an eight-year-old schoolboy. The same giggling I did when my friend typed *58008* on a calculator, turning it upside down to reveal *BOOBS* in the middle of a lesson. I was told off by the teacher, and then I immediately felt anxious, with a knot in my stomach.

It's not entirely happenstance that the same thing was happening in the session with Tim.

Was I biting the breast?

I'm still not entirely convinced of that. Certainly not Tim's, anyway. But it did highlight that my early emotional patterns and responses could surface under different conditions, including both inside and outside of the therapy room.

While the work with Tim didn't quite go as I had initially hoped, I kept my foot firmly on the emotional brakes for a long time. I also placed him on a pedestal and likely frustrated the hell out of him on several occasions.

Psychodynamic therapy didn't resolve my OCD obsessions, but it gave me something valuable, reflective and enduring. In particular, being able to examine my interpersonal processes in depth. Helping me to understand what I do and why I do it.

This isn't to say that I wanted to change everything about myself. Of course, there were problematic patterns; who doesn't have those? But there were also positive aspects of myself that I wouldn't typically afford any emphasis to, and therapy helped me to develop those parts as well. It helped me to see the wood for the trees, where I was getting in my own way, and where I might be getting in the way of others.

Tim appears in my mind regularly, even several years on. I still think fondly of both him and my experience of therapy. I also continue to be very grateful for his influence in my personal life, as well as shaping my knowledge and career.

That work has also been absolutely crucial in my clinical practice, particularly with clients whose interpersonal process leans heavily into externalising blame. There can be complex dynamics to navigate, and sometimes these are very challenging to work with.

8
Warheads

Knowing your own darkness is the best method for dealing with the darknesses of other people
– Carl Jung

I t's absolutely exhausting being brilliant at everything.

Sasha recoils slightly, then laughs with the pressure and pace of an AK-47 assault rifle.

"I'm joking, Jamie—*obviously.*"

But she's not joking—*not really.*

For a moment, I'm torn between curiosity and trying to park my irritation. When I was a teenager, one of our family dogs was a posh little terrier registered with the Kennel Club as *Sir Martin Donald James.* Thankfully, I drew the long straw and avoided any need for a deed poll. We called our little aristocrat Jamie to save identity confusion.

Naturally, people use variations of names, sometimes terms of endearment. Older adults or people with relatives called Jamie have made accidental slips over the years.

This was not the case with Sasha; it was intentional. She wasn't aware of the personal connection to separating myself from my childhood dog; it had no bearing on her therapy. Yet, we had been working together for the past five weeks, and I expressed a preference to be called James numerous times.

"You must remind me of a childhood friend. Yes, that's it. I just can't quite place them. It suits you, though; you're definitely a Jamie— you should change it!"

"I should change my name?"

She fires off another round of laughter.

Sasha was in her early forties, wore a permanent smile, was mostly cheerful, and always laughed, regardless of the topics discussed. This piqued my interest from our first session about her emotional management.

She had been a senior university lecturer in the Faculty of Art and Humanities for many years. Following a restructure at work and not being happy for a while, she recently took voluntary redundancy. Her mother sadly passed away a couple of years prior, and she inherited the estate.

Using the financial cushion as an opportunity to change her career direction, she signed up for an entry-level counselling course. The intention was to complete this so she could access the psychotherapy programme that the university was offering.

Sasha had been telling me about the mark she received on a recently submitted reflective assignment. The feedback from her tutor was that it was "highly academic-sounding" but didn't demonstrate a sufficient depth of understanding to achieve the required marks. Sasha disagreed. "I'm a very reflective person." Raising this with the course tutor, they maintained the grade but gave in-depth guidance for resubmission.

This happens quite frequently with trainee therapists, particularly when they haven't encountered these types of concepts before. Naturally, when you are working with the complexities of human personalities, you need to have the ability to think flexibly. Consider both your strengths and limitations as well as your own potential impact on others. Reflective skills can take time to build. This is also an ongoing process through clinical supervision and, in many cases, personal therapy.

However, Sasha wasn't happy about the mark.

—At all!

She escalated a complaint to the Head of School. Rather than revising the essay, she spent two days perfecting an email outlining how the original submission categorically met the marking rubric. She also pointed out that she had a PhD and had taught master-level students for fifteen years. She had researched the tutor online from their private practice website.

"They are qualified to bachelor's level only."

Confident that she had a watertight argument, Sasha did not feel it necessary to resubmit, instead citing paragraphs from the regulatory body. This had left her feeling exhausted.

As she is telling me this, I'm starting to think about how much potential pain Sasha might be masking and how she might also be a source of pain for others. Although I wasn't party to the experience she was describing, I have been in her tutor's position on more than one occasion. Having a university student attempt to annihilate your reputation because they're pissed off with their grade isn't much fun.

From how she describes the experience, I also get the sense that she has limited reflective skills. This can change, but it requires someone to be willing to examine themselves and their actions in depth. Particularly for an aspiring psychotherapist, this is crucial for *fitness to practise*.

Apart from maintaining our emotional well-being, we also need to consider our own impact on clients. This includes understanding our reactions and responses. It's particularly important in a therapeutic setting. Problems can easily arise that involve our own processes and personality.

I started thinking about how Sasha might experience rejection from the course if they believe she is not ready for professional training. How might that impact her?

These are all momentary thoughts, and my attention quickly shifts back to what is happening between us in the room.

* ✳ *

When Sasha first approached me, she didn't consider herself to have a mental health problem but felt very lonely since her mother died. Personal therapy was also mandatory as part of the psychotherapy course she was aiming for. She wasn't quite there yet but wanted a head start and had been seeing a female therapist for three months already, which hadn't gone well.

"It was all very businesslike, drawing things all the time. She told me it was all my fault and I wasn't *ready for therapy*—apparently (laughing)."

Her aims for the work with me were very vague. Which isn't so uncommon; lots of people struggle to know where to begin. However, by session five, all I really knew was that she was an only child, her father died when she was young, and her mother died recently. She felt bullied in every job role she held, mostly experiencing this with female colleagues.

After the first session, Sasha very quickly started raising superficial complaints each week. Minor flaws and faults with the building. Issues with the therapy room. "I can see weeds growing from the wall outside that window!" The sofa was too firm and too low. There was no coffee machine.

Even the slightest pressure to consider her own role in the workplace dynamics would lead to redirection, as she analysed her previous therapist. "It's clear that she was gaslighting me, Jamie—don't you think?" Then, visibly irritated when I closed this down, asking about her feelings in the room with me.

It was becoming clear that while Sasha was somewhat armour-plated on the outside, there was quite a lot of emotional fragility underneath. With this type of client, even mild pressure on suppressed feelings can lead to the nervous system shutting down, resulting in a form of emotional decompensation.[1]

Yet, if there is no confrontation, therapy may stall, or emotions and feelings linked to a distorted self-image can become reinforced. Where possible, it's important to attempt to create conditions where emotion can be named and explored. It is often one of the most important steps in helping clients with these types of sensitivities. Naturally, they also need to consent and be willing to do this.

Treatment often requires a slower pace in these cases, gradually increasing exposure to strong emotions. This also involves helping the person to build their capacity to weather inevitable ruptures to the therapeutic relationship.

It can be a tricky balancing act.

* * *

While Sasha's case is fictionalised, it depicts the extreme end of a realistic challenge with perfectionism, where the person holds a generous side plate of entitlement and grandiosity. Although it is rare to come across truly narcissistic patients in mainstream practice, it's more common to encounter what psychodynamic therapists might refer to as *fragile narcissistic defences.*[2]

Sometimes, core beliefs around entitlement develop when a child is excessively idealised or overly praised without realistic, grounded feedback. Although affirming a child's value and worth is developmentally important, consistently framing this as superior or "exceptional" can cause problems in developing a balanced self-appraisal. When caregivers struggle to model humility or acknowledge personal limits, the child may internalise a distorted view of themselves, feeling excessively deserving or exempt from ordinary expectations.

Over time, this can contribute to strategies that mask underlying difficulties and conditional self-valuing.[3] Without opportunities to integrate both strengths and limitations, they may grow intolerant of envy, failure, or criticism.

However, suppose a child grows up in an environment where praise is only offered when they demonstrate that they are "exceptional". In that case, the child may develop a fragile sense of self-worth tied to achievement or superiority. When ordinary performance is met with criticism, humiliation, or rejection, the person may start to associate failure with shame and emotional threat.

This can lead to them internalising harsh expectations and developing a low tolerance for critical feedback.[4] Often, it can be projected onto others as a way to rid themselves of underlying vulnerability and persisting feelings of inadequacy.[5]

Although many people with internal demanding standards can spend relentless amounts of time in the pursuit of avoiding criticism, judgment, and shame, no one can ever be all things to all people. Yet, sometimes, there can be aspects of their behaviour that occur outside of their conscious awareness.[6] Whether they are blind to it or prefer not to look at it.

Inevitably, where this impacts other people, the person can end up drawing the very criticism and judgment that they are working so hard to avoid. Therapy is an opportunity to discuss this in a controlled environment. Naturally, this involves exploring what is happening within the therapy relationship to better understand what is happening outside the room.

Yet, where someone may sense the firmly bolted lid beginning to pop off their feelings of anger, envy and *murderous rage*, they can perceive even the minutest attempt to address the dynamic as an imminent attack. Taking the threat level straight to DEFCON ONE. Anger begins to leak out indirectly through sarcasm, passive-aggressive comments, and subtle undermining[7]. And occasionally—calculated attacks.

This can also feel confusing and unpleasant to the people around them. When a person's process is characterised by constant complaining, criticism, and attempts to control, it can lead to long-standing problems in their relationships. They may be avoided, feared, or matched with criticism and counter-attack. Either way, the person can feel consistently victimised and isolated, with chronic feelings of loneliness.

Anger and rage are not necessarily problems in themselves in terms of the therapeutic process. In fact, strong emotional expression is actively encouraged; it just needs to be containable so that it is not physically acted out. As therapists, we generally invest a lot in our clients, and at times, we have to field criticism and verbal assaults, but not to the point where we are happy to be physically punched in the face.

Like all emotions, anger serves an important function. It lets us know when a boundary has been crossed or when we encounter mistreatment or injustice. However, for some, particularly those with early histories of criticism, emotional neglect, or unpredictable caregivers, anger and rage can feel particularly dangerous. It can feel frightening and often physically exhausting for clients to sit through a lengthy appointment talking about challenging experiences while suppressing rage.

There is a constant process of monitoring and observing what the person is physically saying and doing and, importantly, what is not being said or done.

In clinical practice, this can naturally present significant challenges for the therapist. On the one hand, they need to understand themselves well enough to navigate the dynamics that are frequently live in the room, not overly personalising things. On the other hand, as with any client, care and compassion need to be offered consistently while also resisting the temptation to comply or collude with the defence system.

The following week, I headed down to reception. The usual staff member had stepped away from the desk. Sasha was early, waiting in the enclosed space between the main entrance and the fob-access door.

She was frantically typing on her phone. I assumed she was messaging me to let her in. This had happened before, and she'd spent the session subtly accusing me of leaving her out in the rain despite being in a heated area inside the building.

She looked visibly upset. When I opened the door, she didn't look up, still absorbed in her phone, her hand raised, palm up. "Hang on! There. Done!"

She brushed past me, clutching her usual refillable coffee cup, and headed straight for the stairs. As we reached the landing, she saw the shared kitchenette just off the corridor.

[Sasha] Can I please use your sink to throw this away?
—I can't even look at it!
[Me] Your coffee? As in, you want to pour it in the sink?
[Sasha] Yes. I want to throw it away. It's disgusting.
—I can't drink that!

I hold the kitchen door open for her. She immediately rips the lid off the cup and launches the whole contents at the sink, turning on the tap full blast, swilling the cup and splashing water everywhere.

[Me] There are paper towels in the cupboard just at the
    side of your—
—*Thump.* Sasha throws the refillable cup in the bin.

Now sighing, holding her hand to her chest, with a smile returning to her face. "Thank you so much. That's better!"

We sit in silence for a little while in my room. Sasha makes momentary eye contact, fidgeting with her hands, then gazes up at the ceiling, squinting.

[Me] You seem upset.

[Sasha] Those beams are very dusty, Jamie; you need to speak to the building manager.

Long silence—composing herself.

[Sasha] So, how have you been. Are you well?

[Me] I wonder what's happening for you right now?

[Sasha] Well—you're giving me a strange response to my question, and I'm now wondering what's happening for you (laughing).

Long silence.

[Sasha] Ah, I see. You want to know about my *feelings*, don't you? Grabbing the low-hanging fruit.

[Me] If I'm being honest, Sasha, I feel a bit stuck. There's a sense of sadness when you are in the room. When I ask you about it, you smile and laugh or redirect. That leaves me feeling confused.

[Sasha] Well—that's quite odd, Jamie. From my understanding, a therapist is meant to validate their patients' feelings, not bring their own stuff into it.

[Me] Can you expand?

[Sasha] You said that I make you feel sad.

[Me] So, when I said that, I sensed you might be covering up your sadness with a smile; what you hear me say instead is, "You make me feel sad." Did I get that right?

[Sasha] Okay, Jamie. I'm lost.

[Me] Would you like me to clarify?

[Sasha] Yes—please do (laughing).

[Me] You arrived here today, clearly upset, mentioning feelings of disgust. Then you throw your refillable cup in the bin, which has seemed important to you each week. "A treat," as you put it. Then, when I draw attention to it and ask you about your feelings, you look up at the ceiling and complain about the dust. Then you deflect and ask me how I am, all while smiling. Hence, I am curious about what happens to you when you are in this room with me.

Long silence.

[Sasha] (yawning) I'm feeling very tired from today, Jamie. I'm not sure I have the energy to discuss this right now.

We sit in silence for a while, unsure whether she wants to continue. Eventually, with tears forming, Sasha begins describing something that happened earlier.

Since starting therapy, she'd taken to visiting a nearby artisan coffee shop. She liked the place and had bought an expensive refillable cup with their logo on the side. The owner usually served her and got her order just right: "Triple shot latte with whole milk and chocolate sprinkles," adding a flourish on top each week, even though it was a takeaway. Not ideal to be wired on caffeine before therapy, but it mattered to her.

Today, it was the school holidays, and the shop was packed. A young woman was working the counter, and in the rush, Sasha's order was made with *oat* milk instead of *whole* milk. She noticed once she'd poured it into her cup while sitting outside.

Frustrated, she stormed back in, cut the queue, and tore into the barista, who ended up in tears. The owner stepped in to remake the drink. Sasha asked him to rinse her refillable cup, but he explained it wasn't allowed for hygiene reasons, but she could use the drainage bar. She demanded a replacement refillable cup.

Things didn't go her way. The options were a refund or a disposable cup. People in line began making rude comments. Sasha took the drink, poured the first one down a grate in the road, and came straight to my office.

[Me] Why did you throw the cup in the bin?

[Sasha] It's no use to me. I won't be going back.

[Me] Can you expand?

[Sasha] It's *terrible* service. Would you go back?

[Me] It seemed important to you up until today. I'm wondering if there is more to it?

[Sasha] I'm not spending money where they treat me like that. Besides, I gave them a one-star review online while you left me outside.

[Me] What was the worst part about it?

[Sasha] How they treated me. All they had to do was to correct their error. This could have all been avoided.

[Me] From your perspective, they made no attempt to correct the mistake with the milk?

Sasha's eyes narrow, and her foot starts tapping on the floor.

[Sasha] Well, I'm reflecting on this now, Jamie. Perhaps I was a tad harsh with the girl who was serving.

[Me] Can you expand?

[Sasha] Maybe she is envious of me? Actually, she's regularly seen me spend a lot of money there.

[Me] You're saying that the person serving might envy your social status?

[Sasha] Well, the owner is usually very attentive, Jamie.

[Me] Do you perceive me in a similar way?

[Sasha] Absolutely not! You don't make me drinks—it's how I ended up in that damn coffee hovel in the first place!

[Me] You may be tempted to throw me in the bin, like your coffee cup.

Sasha starts laughing naturally.

[Me] What do you notice right now?

[Sasha] I actually feel really hot.

[Me] As in, heat?

[Sasha] Yes—HOT!

[Me] Where do you notice that?

[Sasha] (angry tone) I would have hoped you, of all people, would validate my experience rather than just interrogating me about it!

Long silence, Sasha is looking at the floor, tapping her foot.

[Me] What just happened there?

[Sasha] (yawning) Honestly, Jamie, I'm exhausted, and I don't think this is really helping. I'm going to head home and take some time to think about it.

Beyond the content of the story, what is interesting to me is that Sasha notices heat in her body when she is caught off guard, indicating that anger is surfacing. When pressed on this, there is fatigue and yawning. This suggests to me that even mild pressure to explore her feelings has sent her nervous system into shutdown. I attempt to help her regulate this, but she decides to check out.

✳

At this point, you might wonder if therapists are robust, unshakable beings. We're not. Naturally, we are human with normal feelings. I sometimes feel contempt toward Sasha, frustrated by her constant complaining, the public devaluation of other women, and then her positioning herself as the victim. I'd even rehearsed how I might end therapy with her.

However, terminating abruptly with someone so sensitive to rejection would likely confirm her worst fears. Our working alliance is low; she remains in an isolated bubble, even in the room. She doesn't acknowledge my name, let alone really see me. Therapy isn't progressing, and I doubt she could tolerate a tough love monologue without shutting down.

This is why clinical supervision is essential. Supervisors, who are experienced therapists themselves, help us reflect honestly on our work. Therapy isn't confined to the hour we spend with a client; it's supported by ongoing oversight to ensure safety and integrity. I would describe how Sasha leaves me feeling inadequate. "A shit therapist." These are partly what Sasha *transfers* to me, consciously or not. They also brush up against my own sensitivities. One of the core principles of therapy is to acknowledge these feelings and reactions in the client's interest rather than weaponising our insight.

If Sasha has this impact on me in a single hour each week, it's reasonable to assume that other people in her life feel that way, too. What does that mean for her chances of intimacy, friendship, or care? What must it be like to feel so threatened by connecting to someone that your only options are to smile or attack? That's deeply sad. And was the reason I chose to share the dilemma with her.

Sasha's comment about validation is partially true. Many modern psychotherapy approaches place a strong emphasis on emotional validation. However, while all emotions are real in the sense that they are subjectively felt, they are not always valid in how they are interpreted or acted upon. Clients like Sasha often express emotion through complaining, blaming, or displaying superiority. The anger and contempt she is expressing are real to her. Yet, based on the context she has described, these are more likely secondary emotions, distorted by defensive processes and used to shield more vulnerable core states such as shame, guilt, envy, and grief.

Sasha shows low reflective capacity. Even gentle confrontation is met with rationalisation and justification. Where insight is limited, it's clinically safer to stay with the feelings emerging in the room, directed toward the therapist.

Simply validating the narrative risks reinforcing the defences that maintain the difficulties rather than helping the person access the more painful emotions buried beneath, often held in the physical body.

Where trauma is likely, it's essential not to force lids on painful memories, especially where there is no consent to do this. Without sufficient stability and readiness to explore internal experience, adaptive processing is unlikely, and the risk of re-traumatisation increases significantly.

* ✳ *

A few days later, Sasha emailed to say she'd be unavailable for a few weeks due to a training opportunity. She was feeling much better and didn't wish to continue with therapy but wanted a final session to close things down. I assumed she'd found a new therapist, perhaps a better fit. Still, I appreciated her willingness to meet for a final time. Not everyone does. Some people send polite emails, as I did with Gill. Others ghost, metaphorically *murdering* the therapist in their mind. Sometimes we end up on the shelf of marvellous things or in the bin of useless objects. I wasn't sure which route Sasha would take.

She arrived unusually upbeat, practically skipping up the stairs. When I asked how she felt about ending, she told me she'd dropped out of the counselling course and no longer intended to pursue the psychotherapy training. "So I don't need therapy anymore." The external examiner had upheld her mark, and the tutor had commented on her readiness for training. Sasha had looked this up and was livid. "She's literally a glorified counsellor; who the hell does she think she is!"

Instead, she'd completed a brief online course recommended by an acquaintance, built a website, and decided to launch her own business. She was eager to show me her new business card.

Dr. Sasha Brunel, PhD

EXECUTIVE TRAUMA & RELATIONSHIP COACH

Take your first step towards healing with Dr Sasha

DSNT XST Certified Specialist

I shift in my seat with the body posture of a praying mantis, so I take a breath from my stomach. I manage to swear in my head rather than out loud, maintaining an expressionless face.

I am really torn. It's essential to hear from Sasha about her experience with therapy, but I'm also concerned that she's misrepresenting her PhD in culture and heritage to work with vulnerable client groups. Without any formal training, she has the potential to harm both herself and the public. I'm tempted to school her. Yet, working as an unqualified and unregulated therapist isn't against the law in England. There's nothing I can do about it, and she likely wouldn't hear me anyway.

I invite her to give feedback about therapy instead. She pulls out a writing pad and shifts gears. She lets loose. Shaking throughout but composed enough to get to the end of the professional competencies she had printed from the internet.

Sasha was bypassing the bin of terrible things and opting for a slow-paced annihilation—up close and personal. With no time to recover from my injuries, I reply.

"It sounds like your experience was very painful."

I await my inevitable fate as she loads the final bullet.

—A fatal blow.

She places a business card on the edge of my desk by the door.

"My fees are higher than yours, but if you get *stuck* with your other patients, please bear me in mind."

Silenced.

Compelled only to repeat her last word.

Light shines through the window.

The shadow of a weed dances on the seat where she sat.

Both are lost.

9
Containment

A Joy to be hidden; a disaster not to be found
—Donald Winnicott

Few ever imagined that the social world could stop.

At 4.30 pm on Wednesday, 11th March 2020, Dr Tedros Adhanom Ghebreyesus, Director-General of the World Health Organisation, declared the novel coronavirus a global pandemic. Of course, I'd been mentally preparing for this moment since 1995, with images of Dustin Hoffman in the film *Outbreak* still etched in my memory bank. I was working in community-based mental health services in the NHS at the time. When the virus first spread beyond Wuhan, China, my mind was already focused on work. What would happen if it landed in the UK? Where would I source an N95 respirator? Surely we can't do therapy online? I wonder if Amazon sells hazmat suits?

I was sitting at a standstill in rush hour traffic when the announcement from the WHO came over the radio, trying to get home from York. The first UK cases had been confirmed in the city centre at the end of January. The people affected had been isolating in a hotel, and the virus was contained. When it made national headlines, some of my patients experienced notable flare-ups. People with pre-existing anxiety problems were becoming more health anxious, with new compulsions around contamination fears. Those with physical health conditions such as asthma and chronic obstructive pulmonary disease were becoming increasingly cautious, some not wanting to leave their homes.

Despite the naturally growing concern that we were all facing, I was taking it all in my stride. Typically, I only ever really worried about irrational things. When it came to realistic pressures or crisis situations, I've always been quite pragmatic and grounded.

Yet, there was also a part of me that was being somewhat blasé and dismissive. A kind of semi-denial that the predictions I was hearing from medical colleagues were exaggerated. That the distressing images I was seeing on the TV from the hospitals in Italy and Spain would never happen here in England.

I mean, we're British! We had Boris Johnson emulating Churchill on the news. Realistically, we were heading for imminent disaster, and the NHS would likely collapse. Still, it was nothing a bit of bulldog courage and a drop of Scotch in your mug of tea couldn't solve.

Surely?

Despite the grim reality brewing in the background, I had an ethical duty to be present for my patients. Allowing my thirteen-year-old part to start grabbing the reins, spending hours engrossed in BBC news stories and Google searches wasn't going to help with that.

Throughout February, I continued to see patients face-to-face in the GP surgeries where I worked. There was plenty of toilet roll in the loos and hand sanitiser in the rooms, despite people starting to ransack the supermarket shelves. I would open the windows in my treatment room with the heating turned up, but there were many momentary silences and looks of concern if anyone coughed.

In early March, the GPs started arriving to work in scrubs, with me still waltzing around in a cable-knit jumper. Yet, it was still pretty much business as usual. Que sera, sera!

That was until a voice boomed out of my car's speakers. Thankfully, the traffic was gridlocked, as my ears started ringing and I couldn't feel my feet, so I had to use the parking brake.

"In the days and weeks ahead, we expect to see the many cases, the many deaths, and the number of affected countries climb even higher. We are deeply concerned both by the alarming levels of spread and severity and by the alarming levels of inaction."
—*Dr Tedros Adhanom Ghebreyesus quoted in The Guardian, 2020.*

This was officially the dawn of COVID-19. It felt like I had been punched from a blind spot. The cushioned padding of pragmatism suddenly stripped down to the grinding rusty pistons firing up with flashbacks to flesh-eating bacteria. But this was much worse. It wasn't just rare cases during open heart surgery. This was happening to lots of different people; infection rates were rising exponentially, and it was right here, now standing on the doorstep, about to walk in.

I still don't remember how I got home.

MONDAY 23RD MARCH 2020, 8.30 PM GMT

The government announced that the UK was locking down.

When COVID-19 finally arrived, it hit fast and hard. Frontline healthcare workers, including care home staff, were literally knocked off their feet and met with impossible conditions. Stretched beyond capacity.

Medical doctors with decades of clinical experience were now entirely in the dark about how to treat their patients who were presenting with life-threatening situations. Ambulance crews were attending calls from people in critical condition, only to have to queue outside the hospitals due to overwhelming demand in the emergency departments.

Nurses, cleaners, healthcare assistants, and doctors had to reuse single-use masks and wear bin bags as aprons. Critical care units were having to triage based on the likelihood of survival. NHS, third sector and private hospital care staff were also dying, disproportionately affecting people from minoritised groups. Many workers were separated from their families due to the risk of transmission.

Much was being said in the media about their bravery and sacrifice, and the general public was out on their doorsteps clapping and banging their pans on Thursday evenings. But much less was being said about the heavy toll it was all taking on the mental well-being of the people on the frontline. Many had to compromise on standards, facing double-bound ethical dilemmas and experiencing moral injuries that they would carry long after the first wave subsided.

The *Archives of Public Health* published a meta-analysis showing the widespread prevalence of moral injury among healthcare workers during the pandemic.[1] For anyone unfamiliar with the term, it refers to the psychological distress stemming from actions, or inactions, that have significantly violated our morals and values.

What I'm describing here isn't an attempt to make a clunky link to OCD and perfectionism. This was a grim reality for many healthcare workers who had little to no physical, emotional, and psychological resources. What does it mean to do *enough* when people are dying in such high numbers? What do you say to people who are no longer allowed to say goodbye to their families? When you know someone needs oxygen, but a ventilator is being denied, not because you chose to withhold it, but because you literally had no choice?

A major review in *Occupational Medicine* painted a very stark picture. Workers were not just becoming exhausted from physical exposure to the virus, but also the emotional and moral weight of the decisions they were having to make.[2]

On top of all that, some were facing abuse and attacks from a small fraction of the public, conspiracy theorists and those managing through brick-wall denial, accusing the hospital staff of lying about what they were facing.

Unsurprisingly, burnout rates skyrocketed. According to the Centres for Disease Control, by 2022, nearly half of healthcare workers reported being burned out, a sharp rise from 2018.[3] Long shifts, relentless waves of patients, and the absence of adequate support systems wore down even the most resilient. And yet, a lot of healthcare workers believed that admitting exhaustion meant they were failing. Many didn't seek help.

Meanwhile, the services I was working for quickly pivoted to remote working. As therapists, we didn't need to be able to physically examine patients. Leadership teams in NHS England were predicting a "tsunami" of mental health problems, and we were busy getting prepared behind the scenes. The tsunami analogy was quite an accurate description, though. We just didn't realise how much the tide would change.

When I eventually started contacting the patients on my caseload, a few had deteriorated, some with increased suicidal thoughts and worsening low mood due to limited social contact. A study published in 2022 in *Frontiers in Psychology* confirmed that this was also observed more broadly.[4] There were also clients with no prior history of contamination OCD now developing excessive hand washing rituals and wiping the packaging on their groceries with bleach. An article in *Time* magazine reported a similar trend.[5] The intense media coverage resulted in blurred lines between advice, caution and compulsion.

But there was also something unexpected that was happening. A lot of people who had been in treatment were no longer needing services. For some, being furloughed from a job they hated had eased the pressure. The weather had been wall-to-wall sunshine, feeling like an unplanned holiday for some. And for several of the people I was seeing for difficulties with OCD, many thought that the pandemic had become a more level playing field.

Years of feeling abnormal had suddenly given way to a sense of acceptable visibility, an unexpected feeling of relief. People who had long lived with contamination fears or intense health anxieties found themselves, for once, on a similar page to everyone else. Lavishing their hands with hand sanitiser was now expected when entering or exiting a building. No longer hidden or covert. No more comparatively "illogical" or "excessive".[6]

At one point, things were so quiet that we were being asked to potentially redeploy to acute and secure inpatient wards to support the staff shortages due to COVID infections. But demand for psychological services soon returned. My caseload was now filled with traumatised healthcare workers and people who were recently bereaved under complex circumstances. All were struggling significantly. In particular, people with high levels of perfectionism were presenting with severe symptoms of anxiety and depression. Highly structured lives were now curtailed beyond the person's influence. Routines, faith, funerals, and family gatherings, gym sessions, events, moving home, career goals and opportunities. All cancelled, restricted, uncertain or on hold.[7]

Context also influenced how people experienced the restrictions on daily life. People who were living in abusive or unsafe domestic situations faced heightened danger and isolation. The imposed restrictions in the UK trapped people in violent homes, cutting off access to safety and informal support.[8] Police reports have since shown that between March and June of 2020, domestic abuse-related crimes in the UK rose by 7%, with nearly 21% of all offences reported as domestic cases.[9]

Those without stable housing or supportive social networks were particularly vulnerable. Shelters and homeless services closed and reduced their operations, cutting access not just to food and hygiene support but also to essential human contact.[10]

But it wasn't an easy time for therapists either. Despite most of us now working remotely, more insulated from direct exposure to death and critical illness, home working didn't suit everyone.

For some, constantly hearing harrowing stories while sitting in their dining room blurred the boundaries between work and home. Many were unable to switch off. I also knew several colleagues who were struggling to negotiate childcare and homeschooling. The comfortable space of their living room that once served to wash the working day away was now spent doing risk assessments for self-harm and suicide, amongst times table charts and re-runs of *Peppa Pig*. Many were feeling helpless and cut off from their team and colleagues.

Trying to help both healthcare workers and the general public adjust to significant loss and adversity came with a whole new set of challenges. Naturally, the field of psychological therapy had sailed into a storm over uncharted waters.

Cognitive and behavioural strategies were the most utilised and adapted to help people make sense of the atypical circumstances they were facing, often focussing on managing health-related worry and low mood. This included techniques to help people establish "functional equivalence". Mostly, attempting to re-establish and maintain a daily routine by working with opportunities that are available, as opposed to what someone was previously able to access.

Mindfulness-based techniques, although not suitable for everyone, were promoted in many regions as a way to stay grounded in the moment rather than ruminating over the past or spending their entire day worrying about the future. Easier said than done when you're in the middle of a global crisis, but it was helpful for some.

In many of the cases I was seeing, people were struggling with very recent losses complicated by the restrictions. Often, it was too early to intervene with psychological therapy. Healthcare workers were also facing repeated daily exposure to multiple traumas and presenting in acute states of distress.

At times, many therapists, including myself, were struggling to feel that they were able to help. A lot of the work during the early stages of the pandemic involved listening, validation, and emotional support.

And that could be like touching the burning sun.

The concept of *self-care* has been around for some time but gained widespread attention during the COVID-19 pandemic. It's often been promoted in vague or heavily commercialised ways. But the nuts and bolts of self-care are pretty much giving yourself time for rest, putting boundaries in place where necessary, and affording yourself the same compassion you might afford to others.

As you might imagine, if your internal standards are hell-bent on working you into the ground, taking time out to rest and play can feel very uncomfortable. "Lazy!" "Weak!" "Failure!" "Undeserving!" "Guilty!"[11] [12] Rather than responding to their own needs with kindness, many turned to self-criticism, sacrifice, and denying themselves support.[13]

Where people struggle with this, it often requires a radical challenge to our thinking, pushing back against deep assumptions about worth, value, permission, and emotional legitimacy. From my own perspective, this has meant intentionally creating gaps in my week to do something other than work. But that doesn't mean you have to be sitting in bath bombs and rose petals if that isn't your thing.

Although it took some time to adjust, the pandemic challenged some of our prior assumptions. On the one hand, online treatment didn't suit everyone. Particularly, those in poverty had limited access to video-enabled equipment or the internet. On the other hand, for those with access to technology, the pandemic demonstrated that we didn't need to be in the same physical space to connect emotionally.[14]

However, personality also appeared to play a role. For people who naturally preferred a slower, quieter pace of social life, the lockdown brought unexpected relief. Life became calmer and more manageable without the constant pull of invitations, gatherings, or crowded workplaces.

Many were also saving a lot of time and money with their new ten-second commute. Living in safe environments with safe people and relationships. Increased efficiency and flexibility. Access to countryside and gardens. Able to go walking with the dog at lunchtime. Some had spare rooms kitted out as a home office. Admittedly, this was also the case for me.

＊ ✳ ＊

There was an initial settling-in period and some natural anxiety. I worried about my ageing parents, and my sister, an experienced nurse, who may potentially be redeployed to the COVID wards.

While much of the country was repainting walls or planning loft conversions, my mind went straight into rescue mode. How much extra work could I fit into the fifteen hours a week I now had spare?

What I hadn't expected, after decades of worrying about disease and illness, is that I would be someone who thrived during the end of the world. It was also sobering to realise that it took a global shutdown and millions of deaths to give myself permission to rest.

In fact, had it not been for the pandemic, you wouldn't be reading this book. The additional time allowed me to take a radical look at what I was previously doing and shift my perspective. Things I'd previously dismissed due to the hyper-focus on my career were now in play. I discovered writing for pleasure rather than academic submission.

But there were strong feelings of guilt and shame that came with this, and I would keep it to myself during work meetings. A lot of staff members were struggling. We would regularly attend team calls with different therapists, psychologists, and managers. During *reflective practice*, there were nine video tiles on my screen full of solemn faces.

Naturally, I attempted to read the room. It didn't feel appropriate to be bouncing around like Tony the Tiger when I was asked how I was doing.

"I'm GGrrrrrreeeeeeaaattttTT!"

So, I covered it up instead. "I'm *just* about coping."

There was a common assumption that everyone was feeling equally terrible. On the odd occasion when I admitted I was doing well to a colleague or supervisor, it drew inquiry and covert accusation, perhaps a form of defence mechanism. At times, it would leave me questioning whether this was actually the case. I mean, no one in their right mind could possibly prefer the post-apocalyptic social world to the norms we were previously used to? Yet, speaking with many colleagues, friends, and clients since then, it turned out that I wasn't the only one.

For me, it came down to how we connect and the different ways we draw energy from the social world.

We've all heard the familiar message: "Humans are social creatures, and we are built for connection." While I agree with this to a point, the pandemic highlighted just how differently people experience connection. Our personality traits, core schemas, and levels of introversion or extroversion all shape what we find meaningful and, equally, what drains our social batteries and emotional energy.

Introverted people, particularly those prone to anxiety in social settings, seemed to experience genuine relief from the sudden removal of social pressure. Lower physical comparison, or expectations to perform and present in public, feeling safer in their own company.[15] It gave them space to navigate social interaction on their own terms. More able to push back against workplace demands and no longer being watched in an office environment. A few people I knew were reporting reduced burnout, improved sleep, mood, and lowered anxiety due to working from home.

In some cases, this relief was only temporary. As the lockdowns dragged on, prolonged isolation or minimal contact with friends and family left a lot of folk feeling emotionally disconnected. Some began to avoid social contact altogether, eventually becoming more withdrawn.[16] Without meaningful emotional feedback, their self-critical thoughts had more room to take hold. For those who relied on external structure to regulate internal states, the lack of daily accountability made it harder to manage anxious thoughts and resist the temptation to compensate by overworking.[17]

On the other hand, people higher in extroverted traits, particularly those who typically draw energy from regular social interaction, often found the absence of in-person contact more destabilising.[18] This was especially noticeable in people whose perfectionism was socially driven, often positively reinforced by how others perceived them. With less in-person feedback, their internal critic started to pipe up, leading to increased rumination and emotional distress.

But many of us can be both introverted and extroverted. I'm typical of this. I enjoy peace and quiet, and I like my own company. That doesn't mean I'm reclusive. I've always been able to maintain long-term friendships and relationships. When I worked in a large NHS team, I often spent my admin days chatting with colleagues, pushing the actual admin into evenings or weekends. I enjoy talking to people, but when it comes to writing letters or clinical notes, I like a quiet room alone. I just hadn't clocked how much time that added to my day. Working from home gave me the flexibility and control to do both.

Aside from the imposed travel restrictions, the pandemic didn't drastically alter the way I lived my life. It just slowed it down. However, I began to notice that variety, rather than necessarily balanced activity, was key to keeping me well. At the same time, I was also starting to realise just how many hours I'd devoted to working over the years, often at the cost of hobbies, people, and, well—life!

* ∗ *

For a significant number of people, the lockdown felt like a painful rupture. The absence of social life and physical touch. Mass exposure to death and loss. While this was a shared global crisis, the psychological and social impact on people in the UK varied considerably and was far from equitable. But our own personality, schemas and tendencies, whether we were consciously aware of them or not, also contributed.

As restrictions lifted and life returned to normal, the general public was able to start re-engaging with familiar routines. For the people who had experienced relief from OCD, many noticed a significant relapse of symptoms and pre-pandemic compulsions.[19] There were also a lot of people who were still struggling with the increased symptoms they developed at the start of the pandemic.

Similarly, a high number of those with demanding internal standards soon reverted to overworking, over-commitment, critical self-reliance, and excessive monitoring. Many were also struggling to maintain the behavioural changes they had implemented during the periods of lockdown.[20]

This was true for me as well. Shortly after the pandemic ended, I left the NHS and opened my own practice. It wasn't long before I slipped back into old habits. Working relentlessly long hours, placing unnecessary pressure on myself, and allowing work to dominate once again.

But this time, there was no manager or department head to blame. Now at the helm of my own ship, I had full control over when and where I could pause to refuel and rest. Instead, I set off at full speed, ignoring the same jagged rocks as before—destination unknown.

For people who are used to constantly pushing themselves or prioritising others' needs, changing pace isn't simply about logistics; it means confronting our internal blocks. Cognitive insight alone is rarely sufficient to shift repeated behaviours and deeply rooted beliefs about worth, value, and achievement. Realistically, long-term change requires consistent alternative action. Otherwise, even the most potent realisations can fade once we return to high pressure or familiar contexts.

But there were some important reminders from a clinical perspective that were highlighted by the pandemic.

Human lives are nuanced. Mental health difficulties rarely appear out of nowhere and stem from many different factors.

There is no universal therapeutic approach when it comes to helping someone overcome their difficulties, nor is there a standard benchmark for how people feel or function.

Still, as uncomfortable as it may be to acknowledge, when we have some degree of influence and control over a problem that we would want or need to resolve, we also carry a degree of personal responsibility to commit to being part of the solution.

10

Unusual Suspects

We shall find courage to assume that there really does exist in the mind a compulsion to repeat which overrides the pleasure principle
—Sigmund Freud

For over a decade, I heard whispers in the NHS.

A mysterious psychological therapy was taking place behind therapy room doors. It was a heavily guarded resource, and experienced therapists were waiting years for state funding to reveal how it was being done. Was it really possible to resolve post-traumatic stress simply by waving your fingers in someone's face? I was sceptical but wanted to find out. After many curious years of waiting, it had finally arrived. This week was the first block of EMDR standard accredited training.

The lead facilitator outlined the stages of the course and what we'd be learning, and there it was—the protocol for OCD. My mind jumped straight back to therapy with Gill in 2012. "So this was actually a thing?"

It would be some time before we got to that, as the early stages focus on single-event trauma. Yet, true to type, I was already thumbing my way ahead through the manual. Until my attention was suddenly pulled back.

> "The best way to learn EMDR is to experience it. So, you'll be working with each other throughout each stage of the training."

—What?!

I was very used to having personal therapy while learning it; this was part of my core training, but never with a stranger delivering a potent trauma treatment with another person watching. Besides, there were around fifty of us on the course, all experienced counsellors, psychologists, and psychotherapists. We were told to keep it "light" and to be mindful of potentially opening a can of worms with each other. "Maybe use personal phobias or recent work stress."

But still, I had read that all sorts of stuff can start surfacing once you're processing. The trainer had already explained that it was pretty common for the mind to start tracing itself further back in time once the memory network was accessed.

What would happen if there was a dark skeleton buried somewhere in the vault of my memory bank? If I started having a strong reaction, what would people think of me?

There was a nagging doubt.

During the extensive therapy I did with Tim, I struggled to recall anything before the age of twelve, and absolutely nothing before I was eight. Also, typical of a lot of people who experience health anxiety, I was sensitive to internal physical changes in the body, having learned this the hard way.

Any time I attempted to "focus on my breath" during the numerous Mindfulness-based sessions at various work events, it would throw my breathing off. Twice, this induced hyperventilation and panic, feeling unable to breathe.

From what I had learned during my time working in trauma services, these were all potential indicators of someone who had been traumatised, at least from a textbook understanding of it. But I didn't have any point of reference.

I also knew from the work that I did with Gill that one of my schemas was *harm and illness*. This had always centred around house fires, terminal illness and death, but no obvious early memories linked to this, certainly nothing that met the criteria for PTSD.

So what was I worrying about?

At best, it would be an opportunity to experience EMDR first-hand. At worst, I would unlock a box that my subconscious was keeping tightly shut and start having a meltdown in front of new professional colleagues.

Great!

What I did not know at the time was that this would be the catalyst for a seismic shift in my clinical practice.

* ✳ *

For anyone who has never heard of it before, eye movement desensitisation and reprocessing (EMDR) was developed by Francine Shapiro in the late 1980s after a random discovery while walking through a park. She had been thinking about troubling thoughts and realised that her eyes were rapidly moving from side to side at the same time. But something peculiar seemed to occur. The associated disturbing feelings generated by the thoughts had now reduced, in fact, pretty much neutralised them altogether.

It was all a bit strange; maybe it was happenstance?

Given that Dr Shapiro was a researcher, very much about the science, she began trying to replicate this with willing colleagues. It transpired that it wasn't just the eye movements that were reducing strong feelings; even tapping on each side of the body or sounds moving from ear to ear had a similar effect. Cutting a very long story short, nearly four decades of research later, EMDR is now a well-established trauma therapy across the world and is a recommended first-line intervention for trauma in the NHS.

If you're now trying to move your eyes from side to side, it's not quite that simple. EMDR involves a detailed assessment, and there is a structured way of identifying and setting up a target memory. It also needs to be done with a trained professional. Without the right support, people can become overwhelmed by flashbacks or intense emotions and may need help staying grounded in the present.

So, what happens with EMDR for OCD?

How does it work?

The underpinning concept is something called *adaptive information processing* (AIP).[1] It's based on the idea that our brains have a natural tendency to recover from tough experiences in a similar way to how our body responds to a cut or bruise. Given a bit of time and the physical body doing what it needs to do, in most cases, it heals on its own.

This is the same if we experience emotionally traumatic events. With enough support and perspective, our brains will adapt over a few weeks or months.

However, if the circumstances are very overwhelming, life-threatening, or we experienced them alone or without help, sometimes it doesn't always fully *digest*.

When that happens, parts of the memory, such as the emotions, images, beliefs, or sensations in the physical body, can stay stuck in the past. They can become reactivated in situations that feel similar and *trigger* the stuck parts of the memory, causing the body to respond as if it were happening again. If this happens early in life, especially if it's repeated, it can significantly impact how we perceive ourselves and the world around us.

EMDR helps someone to revisit these stuck experiences in a controlled way and reprocess them effectively. Using eye movements and *bilateral stimulation*, the memory goes from feeling like a current threat to something that's in the past, no longer fuelling our thoughts and emotions.

While this all sounds very plausible and a tad scientific, most EMDR therapists will readily admit that we don't really know how or why it works. Still, we encounter a wide range of clients with diverse issues, yet many achieve similar outcomes and results.

And not just with PTSD.

Although EMDR is not considered to be a first-line treatment for OCD here in the UK, it is regularly used in private practice. However, the evidence base is still emerging, and there isn't a tremendous amount of research behind it at the moment.

There have been a small number of clinical trials, including case reports showing significant reductions in symptoms where the onset of OCD is clearly linked to specific traumatic or adverse events.[2] For example, someone whose compulsive rituals began after a serious illness or bereavement.

Adaptations of EMDR have also been developed to focus more directly on early relationships, as well as intrusive imagery, shame, or moral injury. In some cases, clients have targeted harsh self-critical beliefs underlying obsessive thoughts and images, which has led to improvements in anxiety and compulsions.[3] This also includes people who haven't responded to standard exposure-based intervention.[4]

While these findings are encouraging, they remain relatively limited. It's also unclear whether EMDR directly reduces obsession and compulsion or if it mainly helps by easing the anxiety and emotional intensity that come with them.

That said, many therapists report finding it helpful in their clinical work. In my own practice, I often combine EMDR with CBT and have found that clients tend to engage more readily with an integrated approach than with CBT alone. Of course, no therapy is a perfect solution, and challenges can arise regardless of the methods that we use.

＊ ＊ ＊

We were now halfway through the first week of training. I was playing it safe, using a minor issue at work for the practicum.

So, which skeletons revealed themselves?

—None!

In fact, nothing at all happened, apart from my eyes going a bit blurred trying to follow umpteen floating balls and telescopic pointers when the person's arm was getting tired. I was starting to resign myself to the likelihood that after all these years of therapy, perhaps I was truly "treatment resistant".

Generally, I'm the sort of person who gets overexcited about training courses. If you've ever been stuck waiting to leave because someone kept asking lots of questions at the end, made you miss your train, or you were late for the school run—that was probably me.

Not this time, though.

During the end-of-day discussion, most people were sharing deep insights, personal revelations, and moments that connected all the way back to their childhood. It was interesting to listen to. I just sat there, looking miserable.

Admittedly, I was pretty disappointed.

As the week went on, I realised I was running into something I often see in my own clients.

First, I was putting way too much pressure on myself to come up with something meaningful. Getting stuck in the worry that the eye movements would stop and I'd be left with nothing to show for it. Second, I kept dismissing random thoughts and images, trying to force them back to what I thought I *should* be focusing on. And finally, a common blocking belief. "I'm not doing it properly!"

EMDR is possibly one of the few therapies where the role of the clinician is to stay as far out of the way of the client's process as possible. Equally, trying to help the client stay as far out of their own way as possible and just "go with it".

No ethereal light was coming out of the clouds, and no huge surge of memories or revelations. By the end of the week, I decided to go all in, bringing my vulnerability to harm and illness schema to the table.

Using a current health worry about a random sore spot on my gums, we put this into *flash forward*, and off I went.

—Again, nothing.

I couldn't hold the image. Just the sensation of someone dragging a hot poker up the length of my body, with pins and needles in my arms, neck, and one side of my head.

At that point, I started wondering if the eye movements had triggered a stroke—very on-brand for the schema, which intensified the feelings.

> [Trainee] Take a deep breath from your stomach. What do you get now?
>
> [Me] Still the same, struggling to hold it, no change. But the physical stuff is increasing.
>
> [Trainee] Good. Just notice what's happening in your body and go with that.

With around ten minutes remaining of the practicum, a single image emerged. I was in a living room in an unfamiliar house, describing the layout, the pattern on the carpet and a cream leather sofa. Then, I could see a little dog wrapped in an orange towel. The unpleasant sensations in my physical body were becoming even more intense and uncomfortable.

—And that was that!

We were asked to rejoin the main room for discussions to close down the final day of the first stage of training.

This time around, people were sharing quite intense feelings of gratitude. Some had apparently resolved major childhood traumas in the space of a couple of days despite already having had years of personal therapy.

As a therapist, I found it moving, and I was genuinely pleased for them. But I was exhausted. My body felt like it had been clamped in a vice, and I didn't think my single image of a dog would be a particularly compelling encore.

It would be another three months of clinical practice before we would all meet again.

* ✳ *

The following week, I went across to see my mum for lunch. Curious to test out if the whole *dog in a blanket* saga was an actual memory or just simply an invention of my mind. I suspected the latter but decided to ask her about it anyway.

[Me] Might sound strange, but why would I have a memory of a living room (describing it)?

[Mum] Our first house was laid out like that. You were only two years old when we moved out, though. I doubt you will remember it.

[Me] Apparently, I do.

[Mum] I've got a photo of you standing on that sofa. It's probably this you're thinking of rather than a memory.

[Me] It is. But there was also a little dog lying on a bed, wrapped in an orange towel.

[Mum] —Oh! (slightly shocked) That was Monty, our first dog. He was attacked by a pack of local dogs that one of the neighbours had let roam free.

[Me] This was at the first house?

[Mum] Yes. The dogs managed to get into our garden. Your dad was at work, and we didn't have a phone. I was on my own with you, and no one could help me get him to the vet. He died.

[Me] What about the orange towel?

[Mum] I put that underneath him because he was bleeding. Your dad buried him in it when he got home.

Although it was a sad story, and difficult to make sense of why it had come up on the back of an irrational health worry about my gums, I was quite excited. Was this a touchstone memory that I had been learning about in the training?

Never being one to wait around and always completely obsessed with understanding things, I checked into therapy.

Mark was a clinical psychologist. He was my fifth therapist, and at the time of writing, he was also the last.

Before we started, I'd spent a fair bit of time thinking about the specific schema domains I wanted to explore through EMDR. We agreed to assess each target as we went along and worked together for a couple of months.

The tricky part was that, after years of therapy, training, and a lot of reading, I already had my own formulation mapped out in some detail. Letting go took time, but when I finally did, what emerged wasn't quite what I'd anticipated.

The fear of harm and illness had always been the most intrusive theme in day-to-day life, so that's where we began. I'd always assumed it came down to early modelling—learning to worry about my health from my mum. That was partly true. But there was a lot clustered around it.

We started by setting up the first target. This was a future scenario of my dentist finding oral cancer.

Again, it took a while to get going. Eventually, my brain seemed to throw itself into reverse. I was back in our first house, Monty on the orange blanket, and the same physical sensations shot up through my back, neck, and head. I was sceptical, of course, about whether I was genuinely accessing this memory or just steering myself there. Still, I followed Mark's instruction to "Go with it—notice that."

Then it got strange. A burning sensation started in my chest, sharp and unpleasant, like acid reflux.

Two images flickered up. The first was a brown cup sitting on the kitchen worktop in the family home I grew up in, but seen from below as if I were looking up at it. The second was harder to place: a small room with cream walls, a small overhead light and what looked like faint blue flashes. It didn't make sense.

Later, Mum filled in the blanks. When I was very young, my dad left watered-down bleach in a mug to remove the tea stains. He went to work and forgot to move it. Somehow, I'd managed to reach it and drink it. Dad was at work. There was no one to help. Thankfully, this time, we had a phone. I was blue-lighted to the hospital in an ambulance. Mum had been pacing up and down, frantic and in a state of panic.

—You're noticing a theme?

Thankfully, it was rubbish bleach and watered down so much that it simply upset my stomach for a couple of days.

Then came a flurry of memories. Mostly fragments, small mini-movies at times. Arriving one after the other, in no particular order.

Our old family dog, *Jack*, who was blind, wandered through the garden gate after a relative left it open. He was hit by a car on the road outside but somehow survived.

The night our neighbours had been burgled. Another where someone had died. I remembered my parents whispering about it all in the kitchen. Like most children, I had the ultrasonic hearing of a bat. I caught every word. Tightness in my chest and a breathless feeling arrived as I was recalling it. I could even see the 1970s hearth I was sitting on.

—Where on earth was all this coming from?

An overnight stay in the hospital, having my adenoids out. Limited visiting hours and being scared to interact with the other children, staying in my bed, wanting to go home.

Riding my Chopper bike with my little sister perched on the back, she would have been about four. I hit a rock, and she fell, hitting her head and ending up with a concussion. I could see myself sitting on the fourth step of the stairs, looking at my parents' worried faces. I was convinced she was going to die, and it was all my fault.

Aged nine, one of the classrooms at school caught fire due to an electrical fault. We were all lined up on the playground, waiting for the fire brigade, billowing smoke and frantic teachers. I could taste the distinct chemical smell of burning plastic at the back of my throat.

Happy memories came through; my parents set up a Spider-Man tent in the living room on Christmas morning. This was the year I got the TV that I compulsively pressed. Adrenaline-filled holidays in water parks and snowboarding with my dad.

It went on for three long sessions.

---

* * *

So, was this the brand new Rolls-Royce of psychotherapy, shining a light through years of OCD?

Not exactly.

EMDR is better described as a clinical technique than a traditional therapy model. It doesn't rely on insight, narrative coherence, or a long-term therapeutic relationship in the way many classic approaches do. From my perspective, the AIP model integrates many of the existing theories.

From a theoretical standpoint, most of the major models are still visible and relevant. Carl Rogers' emphasis on *following* the client, underpinning person-centred counselling. His belief that, when given the right conditions, humans possess an innate drive toward growth that he called the *actualising tendency*.[5] The main difference with EMDR, is that the conditions for growth aren't strictly dependent on the therapist-client relationship. You do need to establish safety and trust early on, but the clinician's job is more about helping the client straddle dual awareness, one foot in the past, one in the present, and the brain does most of the heavy lifting.

Psychodynamic ideas are also highly relevant, particularly in relation to defences and object relations, internalised helplessness, and absence. Rather than working with these interpersonally, the eye movements, or bilateral stimulation, seem to bypass those blocks, and the associated emotions are processed and integrated with the memory.

The cognitive model stands up here, too. There are definite shifts in beliefs and appraisals that become more adaptive. Concepts from Gestalt theory are also applicable, particularly the idea of reintegrating parts of the self that had previously felt fragmented or disjointed.

Was I now able to keep a rational perspective, calmly attending the routine health check I'd been avoiding?

Sort of.

I was absolutely fine at the dentist, but I didn't realise that I wasn't anxious until I left. Since having EMDR, I haven't experienced a flare-up of irrational health worries or any spirals of excessive anxiety. But it's not until I actually think about it that I notice the absence of it.

Sadly, this was not the case with the compulsions. I would just find myself standing in the kitchen before leaving for work, checking the oven hob and looking at the gas taps.

No longer lost.

Calm as a cucumber.

Still on repeat.

Same with the house, car, and office doors. Still a strong urge to check, tap and touch. I would catch myself balancing things out without realising I was doing it.

Maybe my brain was susceptible to wiring itself into habits after all? Perhaps a neurological quirk? Neurotransmitters? All of the above? Who knows.

Mark did explain that EMDR for OCD is usually combined with response prevention. Admittedly, that took a bit of thought. It was quite a strange thing to be doing ERP without the need for exposure.

Yet, I was also finally convinced that after all the avenues I had ventured up, I wasn't going to find any definitive answers as to how or why my OCD started. There was a melting pot of possible factors, and it wasn't necessarily anyone's fault, including mine. The only way I was going to resolve it was through intentional action in the here and now.

Which meant I also had to eat a rather large shit sandwich.

Having idealised particular models of therapy over the years and shunning behaviourism for over three decades, here I was, back to basics—actively engaged in habit reversal.

Granted, my experience as a client was less typical than what I see in general practice. I already had a considerable amount of knowledge about myself from prior therapy, as well as a working understanding of the clinical process. It still wasn't easy, but I was highly motivated for the work with concrete goals in mind. That isn't common with people in therapy for the first time.

Yet, while I'm still occasionally doing some checking, tapping and balancing, there has definitely been a shift. I can lock my house, car, and office doors, check the handles once and leave them without thinking about it.

That's taken decades.

It was a significant win.

11

New Blood

9.30 am on a cold Friday morning in February

The overnight snow caused problems on the roads.

I arrived at the office later than I usually would, which threw me off, and I didn't have my usual admin time. Cranking the heating up high to quickly warm the room, I reviewed the referral note for my first appointment.

Tobias Burton-Smith (34)
Preferred name: Toby

Hi, I've had lifelong problems with anxiety and OCD with a recent flare-up since the birth of my daughter. I've had CBT before and I would like a different approach. There's possibly some childhood stuff as well. If you think you can help me, I would appreciate a discussion.

During a brief call with Toby ahead of his first session, he explained that his wife had experienced a medical emergency during the birth of their daughter, Lucy. Both had remained in the hospital for some time.

Toby had experienced OCD flare-ups before and received CBT at university for contamination fears, but nothing as severe as this before. As his wife and daughter's discharge date approached, his cleaning rituals escalated. Once they arrived home, he started scrubbing his skin raw, applying household bleach, and then rinsing it off as soon as it began to sting. He was also refusing to touch his wife or baby without gloves.

He said this was to protect the baby's skin from any residual bleach. But the situation had already reached a crisis point. He'd been living in a hotel for three weeks, unable to cope at home. The financial strain had finally pushed him to seek urgent support.

Just before 10 am, I went to reception to meet him. Toby was wearing a padded winter coat and gloves, still dressed that way as he sat down, despite the near-tropical temperature of the room. I invited him to use the coat stand, but he declined, saying he'd been anxious all morning and was sweating heavily in the car. He quickly overheated and eventually removed the coat and gloves. The skin on his hands was cracked and raw, with pale blotches up his forearms. It looked like he'd been doing a surgical scrub with bleach. I made a mental note but held off commenting. I wanted a fuller picture first.

Toby had a good intellectual grasp of OCD and spoke about his earlier experiences, but said he hadn't been able to manage the rituals this time.

He originally trained as a biomedical engineer and now led a research team at a tech company. The product they were developing, if patented, could secure him financially for years to come. Although he was entitled to paternity leave, he hadn't taken it. "Lucy arrived earlier than expected, and there's no way I can take the time off right now."

[Me] Do you have any sense of how this all started?

[Toby] It got bad after my wife had the transfusion.

[Me] Blood transfusion?

[Toby] There were complications; she lost a lot of blood.

There is a long silence, and Toby starts struggling to speak.

[Me] What's the worst part about it all?

[Toby] I can't get the thoughts out of my head that my wife is infected with HIV. I didn't say anything, but she could tell something was wrong.

[Me] You're worried the blood the hospital gave your wife was contaminated? Is that right?

[Toby] Yes. I know it's a very small risk because of the screening process, but she couldn't breastfeed as her milk hadn't come. I told my wife that I thought it would be best to keep Lucy on formula.

[Me] Because of the risk of transmission?

[Toby] Again, I get it's a slim chance. But they were both recovering well. The midwife even said that it wasn't an issue if she had to stay on formula.

[Me] Then what happened?

[Toby] I arrived at the hospital one evening to see them after I'd left work.

Long Silence. Tears start streaming down his face.

[Toby] My mum was sitting with her arm around my wife while she breastfed Lucy. I know how important it was to her, she'd been really upset. But it can take over a week for the viral load to show up on a blood test. Why take that kind of risk so soon?

Clenching his fists and jaw, tears still streaming.

[Me] What do you notice in—

[Toby] —I hate her for doing it. I just can't believe she would risk infecting our daughter. I know it makes me sound unreasonable. But I just feel so disgusted. Like, I want to rip my own skin off (rubbing his arms).

Toby understood the irrational nature of his fear to some degree, but he couldn't overcome it. He had persistent thoughts that any bodily fluids: urine, faeces, saliva, or vomit, might contaminate him. Obviously, all of this is entirely unavoidable with a newborn baby.

His wife was being supported by her parents, as well as by Toby's mother and stepfather. But his absence from the family home was starting to cause friction, along with angry remarks from his biological father. "You're a dad now, Toby. This isn't the time to be doing all this again. You need to get your shit together and man-up!"

* ✳ *

It's common for new parents to feel overwhelmed, especially with their first child. The sudden increase in responsibility, combined with sleep deprivation, new routines, and constant care demands, often places strain on relationships and heightens anxiety or low mood.

OCD symptoms can emerge for the first time after a baby is born, often referred to as *Postpartum OCD*. For those with a prior history, it can also trigger significant flare-ups or the return of previously managed symptoms. The content and themes of the intrusive thoughts can also change. This isn't surprising, though, given that a heightened sense of responsibility is a common feature of OCD more generally.

Postpartum OCD affects approximately four in every one hundred new mothers, with some studies suggesting higher numbers when subclinical symptoms are included.[1] New dads or non-birthing partners can also be susceptible to developing it, but it is often less recognised.

Health-related anxieties are common among new parents. Some find themselves constantly hovering over the cot, monitoring their baby's breathing, checking their temperature frequently, or feeling unable to leave them with anyone else.

Contamination fears can also be a significant source of distress, and they can go both ways. Parents may worry about infecting their baby by touching contaminated surfaces, or fear that the baby might contaminate them.

Among new-onset symptoms, the most frequent intrusive thoughts I encounter tend to centre on harm, regardless of gender. These can include graphic sexual images or sudden impulses, such as throwing the baby out of a window, pushing the pram into traffic, or stabbing the child with a kitchen knife. As with OCD more broadly, these thoughts are typically ego-dystonic—deeply distressing and at odds with the person's values. The resulting compulsions are usually aimed at preventing harm, such as avoiding contact with the baby, locking away sharp objects, steering clear of busy roads, or refusing to sit near windows.

In my own practice, I tend to see a higher number of referrals from men, regardless of the issue. Typically, they delay seeking support until symptoms become unmanageable or there is a perceived risk of loss, such as job instability or relationship breakdown. Many try to manage alone for as long as possible, until they reach a crisis point.

There are also added barriers to seeking help with postpartum OCD. As you might imagine, it can feel daunting for anyone, let alone a new parent, to be rocking up to their GP saying that they're having thoughts about molesting or killing their kid. Often, the fear is that this will lead to a referral to social services or the police. Naturally, this can delay them from receiving the right help.

This is why careful risk assessment is essential in any mental health assessment, especially when children are involved. With OCD, the risk of a parent acting on intrusive thoughts is generally very low. Most clinicians familiar with the condition understand that these types of thoughts, in isolation, are not grounds for safeguarding intervention.

However, the potential risk to the parents themselves is often higher. There is growing evidence linking OCD to suicidal ideation, self-harm, and, in some cases, completed suicide.[2] These risks are especially concerning in the perinatal period. They can occur even in the absence of depression or co-occurring psychiatric conditions. While many parents describe their children as a strong protective factor, for some, particularly those experiencing violent or sexually intrusive thoughts, this can fuel beliefs that their child might be better off without them. And it's not uncommon in severe cases. In the past, OCD has often been seen as a "low-risk condition", but it can carry quite serious implications in some cases.

Certainly, when infants are involved, there are also additional considerations. A parent who is overwhelmed by fear and avoidance may struggle to bond with their baby or respond consistently to their child's emotional needs. This can impact a critical window of development in the early weeks and months of a child's life.[3] This is foundational to their sense of safety and connection through interactions with caregivers.

In Toby's case, he did have a history of self-harm, making cuts to his skin with sharp objects. He hadn't done this since university but was now harming himself with corrosive bleach. This meant working with Toby initially around harm reduction. He did experience fleeting thoughts of being better off not being here, but his family were strongly protective, despite the current difficulties. While there were no concerns about the well-being of his daughter, both mum and baby were doing well and had support, Toby was still missing out on a critical time with them both, including his own bond with Lucy.

The next thing we needed to agree on was how we would work together to help Toby achieve his goal of returning home as soon as possible.

Admittedly, new clients sometimes subtly roll their eyes when I mention ERP. Many have tried it before.

Toby gave me a similar look when I explained it would form part of my recommendation, at least in the short term, based on the goals he'd outlined. He had started spiralling into rumination, flip-flopping between blaming himself and accusing his wife. He wasn't responding to my attempts at gently challenging his thinking.

[Toby] My wife's digging her heels in, refusing to have another test. "I'm not colluding with this bullshit," she said. Like that's helpful.

[Me] Were any concerns flagged on the last hospital panel?

[Toby] No, everything came back clear. But those tests don't automatically include HIV anyway.

[Me] It sounds like your wife is actually making a reasonable point there, Toby.

[Toby] (looks surprised) Why would she not just get an HIV test and solve the issue?

[Me] Can I be frank with you?

[Toby] Sure, go for it.

[Me] It isn't your wife's responsibility to be getting blood tests unless she is concerned or there is a medical need for it. Not to ease someone else's worry.

[Toby] Fair enough (looks cross, shrugging his shoulders), I just don't know what else I can do, then. Nothing I've tried works.

[Me] You said earlier that you've done ERP before. Exposing yourself to thoughts of microscopic vomit particles in your room, transferred from the shared kitchen at university? Is that right?

[Toby] (nodding while subtly rolling his eyes)

[Me] What happened?

[Toby] You mean not wiping the surfaces or my hands?

[Me] Yes. Not engaging with compulsions.

[Toby] It didn't work, though, I just ended up sitting there for over an hour with my mind racing and tons of anxiety.

[Me] So, how did you manage to reduce the rituals?

[Toby] My housemates were really supportive, actually. We clubbed together and bought big tubs of hand sanitiser. It was almost a trial run for COVID.

[Me] Okay. That's helpful to know. So, response prevention also applies to compulsions by proxy, as in, not involving other people to do them on your behalf.

[Toby] That may be so, but this is just one more blood test. I'm not asking my wife to start bleaching her hands.

[Me] I imagine if your wife were to agree to another test, it probably wouldn't stop at "just one more"?

Long silence.

[Toby] (laughing) I *very* reluctantly see your point. So, I guess you're suggesting doing ERP *again,* then?

[Me] I genuinely appreciate that this isn't easy for you, Toby. However, I do think that if we can help you alleviate some of the pressure, combined with some key principles, that may give you a better chance of achieving your goals.

Since many of Toby's compulsions stemmed from long-standing issues and he had struggled previously with ERP, we agreed to combine EMDR alongside a structured exposure hierarchy for out of session homework. We started identifying current triggers and future-based fears. Toby chose his first target, and we followed it through until we ran out of road.

After around twenty minutes of working through blocking beliefs. "This doesn't work!" "I don't think I'm doing it right!" He began noticing physical sensations: tightness in his wrists and arms, strong nausea, and brief, fragmented images. His mind drifted back to a supermarket car park.

[Toby] That's weird.

[Me] What do you notice?

[Toby] I can see Mum's face in the rearview mirror, not much else. I actually feel quite sick, though. Possibly from moving my eyes? Does that normally happen?

[Me] Does it feel tolerable?

[Toby] Yeah, just nausea, I don't think I'm going to vomit.

[Me] Notice what's happening in your body and go with it.

Continuing with eye movements.

[Me] What do you get now?

[Toby] I'm just wandering off track to random stuff. I think I'm just making things up.

[Me] What do you notice?

[Toby] Not sure—I think Carl (baby brother) and I had a sick bug. It's just a memory of the bucket on the living room floor.

[Me] Just notice your body and go with that.

Continuing with eye movements—Toby's face begins to contort, and he starts weeping.

[Me] What do you notice?

[Toby] It's jumped to me being in my grandparents' garden. There's a yellow swing I used to play on.

[Me] What do you notice in your physical body?

[Toby] Just really sad. No idea why, though. I loved that swing (laughing and crying at the same time).

[Me] Go with that.

Eye movements.

[Me] What do you get now?

[Toby] Just more memories of my grandparents' house (tearing up), my Grandad, bless him. We lost him to cancer. I was only about thirteen, I think.

[Me] Just notice that.

Eye movements.

[Me] What do—

[Toby] —It's all jumping around. I think it's my dad's old flat. It was high up and I could see across the city. I think I lived with him for a while. Not sure how long, though.

[Me] Just notice your body and go with it.

Eye movements.

[Me] Wha—

[Toby]—I've got a really heavy feeling in my chest and legs now. Is that normal?

[Me] Just notice that.

Eye movements.

[Me] What do you get now?

[Toby] Nothing that time, I started thinking about work.

After the appointment, Toby's mother called him to ask how it had gone. She shared her memory of the events linked to the images that had come up.

Around the time Toby was "playing up in the supermarket" she had just separated from Toby's father, and all three of them had caught a stomach bug. His baby brother became seriously ill, developing a rare complication that led to brain swelling and hospitalisation. While she focused on his care, Toby stayed between his grandparents' house and his father's flat. His brother later experienced developmental delays as a result.

His mother hadn't wanted to worry him at the time. "Besides, you loved spending time with your Grandad." Toby couldn't remember much of it, though.

This was starting to make some sense from a clinical perspective, particularly given his age at the time and the circumstances surrounding his brother's illness.

Young children can be particularly sensitive to the sudden or prolonged absence of a primary caregiver. Whether due to parental separation or a sibling being hospitalised, they often struggle to make sense of what's happening. While brief separations are usually manageable, longer ones can lead to emotional problems. Without the language to express it, it will often show up in their behaviour.

At times, the impact is compounded when the caregiver remains emotionally unavailable afterwards, often due to stress or preoccupation. In most cases, it's not intentional, and it's challenging to manage your time if there's no one else at home to support you. But for the child, this can feel like a secondary absence. Most children are resilient, but repeated disruptions can lead to insecurity in their later relationships.[4]

At his follow-up appointment, Toby explained the conversation with his mother, which had surprised him but also increased his confidence in the process. He was starting to become quite fascinated with it, albeit wanting to know how everything worked at each step.

Rather than overly interpreting or analysing the context, with EMDR, we simply go back to the image from the original target and continue to reprocess it. We do this until Toby reports neutral or significantly reduced disturbance in his body.

[Me] Breathe from your stomach. What do you notice?

[Toby] I used to spend hours cleaning my bedroom desk with antibacterial wipes. Is that likely linked to what's happening now?

[Me] Just think about it.

Continuing with eye movements.

[Me] What do you get now?

[Toby] Just more images of high school. I remembered having the whole 'pOCD' thing happening at that time.

I thought me and Carl were going to prison (laughing).

[Me] Go wi—

[Toby] —Actually, that was the year my best friend, Amir, moved to Canada. Wow, did I feel bad about that. He used to write to me, and I cut him off when he left (starts becoming emotional with tears forming in his eyes).

[Me] Notice your body and go with that.

Extended set of eye movements—Toby is expressing a lot of intense emotion, and we keep going until I can see it begins to shift.

[Me] Take a deep breath. What do you notice?

[Toby] (laughing and crying at the same time) I did the same when I left university. The therapist I was seeing said that I threw myself into coursework to avoid thinking about rejection. Do you think that's what I'm doing now?

[Me] Good. Just think about that.

Eye movements.

[Me] What do you get?

[Toby] (tearful) It's just an image of Lucy's face.

[Me] Just notice that.

Eye movements.

[Me] Take a deep bre—

[Toby] —I was thinking about when I was training in my first job after university (laughing loudly, as if noticing irony). I actually supported the data capture systems for one of the pre-exposure prophylaxis trials.

[Me] Just think about—

[Toby]—Those influenced how HIV is managed these days. It felt good to be part of that.

[Me] Good. Go with that; you're doing really well.

Eye movements.

[Me] What do you notice?

[Toby] It's just a crystal clear image of Lucy. The first time I held her in the hospital.

[Me] What do you notice as you're telling me that?

[Toby] Warm (now tearful).

[Me] Where is that located in the body?

[Toby] Across my chest.

[Me] Good. Notice that.

We had initially created a graded plan for Toby to return home. However, following the session, he decided to move straight back in under his own steam. He was still washing his hands excessively, but using liquid soap and water rather than bleach. Although the thoughts of HIV infection had settled, he was not entirely free of contamination fears. His mind began introducing new themes, and he would count the steps in his head from the living room to the bathroom, stopping midway to put his feet together on the stairs.

However, Toby's relationship with his daughter was a strong motivating factor for him. While he had struggled to engage with therapeutic homework in the past, with only himself to consider, he felt more able to work with it now.

The first few weeks were difficult. Although he had managed to return home, he often felt overwhelmed. At times, he would sit alone in the bathroom for long stretches, waiting for the anxiety to subside. He had periods of heightened vigilance, particularly at night, checking Lucy's cot to make sure there was nothing on her sheets that he perceived as unclean. He still avoided using certain parts of the kitchen and washed his coffee cup before using it, despite it being fresh from the cupboard.

Even so, he began spending more time with Lucy, feeding her without gloves for the first time.

His wife remained supportive, but there was still tension. She told Toby that she felt he had not been emotionally present at home for a long time. "It feels more like you're married to your job." Toby would instantly fly off the handle, becoming defensive. "We wouldn't be able to live in this house otherwise!" His compulsions would flare up again, or he would become withdrawn and irritable, or come home later from work. Although Toby's wife was healing well and interested in sex, Toby was also struggling to engage intimately with her.

Toby was beginning to recognise the degree of impact that he had been avoiding thinking about for quite some time. Given the gains he was already experiencing, he felt ready to explore it.

* * *

As I mentioned in the earlier chapters, dynamic psychotherapy includes concepts such as the superego and internalised objects, but it isn't simply a case of one singular thing or another playing out. More often, it's understood as a constellation of internalised figures from early life that may shift within the same session, depending on the emotional context.

In Toby's case, I was sometimes positioned as his mother, perceived as someone who was preoccupied. "I feel like I'm wasting your time, James. You probably have other people on your caseload with much worse problems." At other times, I would take up the sense of his grandfather, a kind and wise presence. Occasionally, I represented his stepfather: well-meaning and trying to help, yet any advice or suggestion would be taken away for analysis and dismissed, preferring to do things his own way.

Most frequently, particularly if there was direct confrontation, I became the projection of his biological father—quick to criticise, unable to handle his problems, with an expectation of rejection and withdrawal. "I bet you regret the day you took me on, don't you?"

I never met any of Toby's family members in person, but based on his accounts, a familiar pattern emerged. His biological father had a tendency to walk away when responsibility increased.

According to Toby, this often coincided with the birth of a new child. His parents separated when he was born, then reunited. Later, when his brother Carl was born, the relationship ended permanently. He also had a half-brother he had never met. His father's new partner remained in Spain when he returned to the UK.

Toby was beginning to realise that some of his own tendencies were being reflected back to him. At first, the similarity with his father had made it harder to recognise.

Over time, he was able to observe the pattern, better separate his own values from it, and understand that he could make different choices.

There were also feelings of grief and resentment in relation to his mother. He had watched her parent his sister in a very different way from how she had raised him and Carl. She had become a grandparent to his daughter, Lucy, and her style now appeared warmer and more available. With time, and from a more adult perspective, Toby recognised that his mother now had experience and resources she simply hadn't had when he was a child. He was able to draw from this in relation to his own parenting abilities, with more room for compassion.

I worked with Toby for two years. There were months where progress seemed slow, or sessions focused on everyday frustrations. As with any client, there were no magical cures or perfect resolutions. Change, particularly when working with deeply embedded schemas, takes time and can be subtle.

I think of it like a railway junction. Small shifts in the track can lead to a very different trajectory further down the line.

In many cases, those changes gain the most ground once therapy ends.

Inevitably, it also means gradually letting go of something.

And sometimes, that is very difficult to do indeed.

12

Precious Things

*Have nothing in your houses that you do not know
to be useful, or believe to be beautiful*
—William Morris

H umans often become attached to material objects.
Some people pursue wealth, valuing designer
furniture, clothes, and cars. For others, it's the small things:
boxes of photographs and keepsakes from significant life
events. It's very common to "have a clear out", declutter
and discard. Some people love rooms filled with stuff; others
prefer minimalism. The value and meaning differ for each of
us. Sometimes people accumulate a lot of stuff, to an excess,
and can find it very difficult to let go of it. This was the case
for an older adult living in Crouch End, North London.

Mr Edmund Trebus was born near Danzig, now part of Poland. After World War II, he moved to England under a resettlement scheme. Establishing a life in the UK, he raised a family and purchased his own home. He was known in the local area as an eccentric chap, regularly seen pushing a trolley, bringing back precious gems that he would find.[1]

Mr Trebus came into the public eye in 1999 as part of the BBC documentary series *A Life of Grime*.[2] He was in his early eighties, living alone, and under scrutiny from the London Borough of Haringey Department for Environmental Health.

His house was in a severe state of disrepair, and the garden was filled with rusty bicycles, scrap metal, and discarded white goods that he had carefully categorised. He was living in a single room in a family-sized home with no electricity or running water. The rest of the house was impassable, packed from floor to ceiling with garbage bags, papers, several decades' worth of household items, and the occasional dead rat.

Accumulating the equivalent of four hundred tonnes worth of items, complaints had been made by his neighbours. His home was considered a biohazard and a risk to public health, and the local authority began clearing his property. However, the value of the items held significant meaning to him beyond what others could see. He responded with anger and disdain, accusing the council workers of stealing from him.[3]

Mr Trebus was vehemently trying to protect his property from the authorities. Despite his slim frame and short stature, he was a force to be reckoned with.

I was in my early twenties at the time, working in credit risk management for a bank. Most of my day was spent restructuring lending for people in financial trouble. Many were facing forced repossession of their homes. It was a tonic to tune in to watch Mr Trebus, waving his walking sticks, asserting his rights and standing his ground. Even when faced with police, council workers and environmental officers exercising a warrant from the courts, he would reply with a sharp quip.

"Stick it up your chuffer!"

It was great television. Millions of us in Britain tuned in each week, and Mr Trebus became an overnight household name.

It was also the first time I had heard the term *compulsive hoarding.*[4] Having since viewed the footage again, some twenty-five years later, I found it uncomfortable to watch. Gaining life experience and clinical insight since it originally aired, I completely understand why the neighbours complained. I could also empathise with the local authority workers who were having to make some really tough decisions, working in "best interests" but against someone's will. Still, it was upsetting to see an older adult who was clearly angry but also highly distressed about his things being forcibly taken away and destroyed without his consent.

+ ✳ +

Hoarding is a related obsessive-compulsive problem but is no longer classified as a subtype of OCD. It's now recognised as *Hoarding Disorder* by the American Psychiatric Association (DSM-5) and the World Health Organisation (ICD-11). Like most psychiatric diagnoses, it is defined by a cluster of symptoms but the severity and insight into the presence of a problem and the impact on daily life vary widely.

The simplest way to understand it is that a person experiences persistent difficulty and distress in discarding things, which can lead to functional, occupational, and physical problems. In more extreme cases, this can also impact public health, and the local authority sometimes has to step in.[5]

Commonly, it involves objects and possessions that have very little, if any, objective value. Naturally, this can be hard to get your head around, particularly if you are someone who can spot a single biscuit crumb on 400 sq ft of beige carpet. Still, many of us have experienced the importance of things that may hold little value to others.

The majority of us will have encountered *transitional objects* at some point in our lives.[6] These can be all sorts of things. Common ones are items such as blankets, soothers, or toys from childhood that helped us transition from dependence on caregivers to developing autonomy in adolescence and young adulthood. If you are a parent, I'm sure either you or someone you know will have dealt with a few tears from a toddler who is tremendously upset when their dummy is posted to Santa.

Sometimes, we can develop an ongoing reliance on material possessions, and letting go of them can be equally tough. At times, they may serve as one of the few remaining things that help us feel close to people we have lost.[7]

Take a minute to think about your most cherished items. Perhaps these are irreplaceable family photographs, jewellery, or letters written to you by relatives who are now deceased. Let's say they're in a big box getting in your way at home, so you put them in another room. Maybe the attic, if you have one. You don't go up there much. It doesn't particularly bother you that you don't see them each day.

All that matters is they are safely tucked away in the house and available if you need them.

So, what would happen if a psychiatrist and environmental health worker turned up at your door with a court order? They insist you have a psychological problem and you must destroy your box of precious items because your neighbours are concerned that it's unsightly and attracting vermin.

How would you feel?

Would you simply accept that you have a mental health issue, apologise and hand over your family photos, jewellery, and irreplaceable letters? Not even the slightest resistance to giving them up?

—Probably not.

Hoarding can present across a broad continuum but also needs to be considered within the context of societal and cultural norms. Collecting things, thriftiness, or frugality is not uncommon, certainly not up here in Yorkshire. In fact, many of us have habits that involve hanging onto stuff. Most households have a kitchen drawer filled with crap. Apologies: used batteries, fuses and plugs from things you binned ten years ago, and birthday candles from the 90s that may "come in handy". My own drawer of crap contains half a tube of superglue that expired three years ago and keys to door locks that have long been replaced from all the pushing and pulling.

But this isn't hoarding. Nor is it about "miserly spending habits" or OCD. The difference is that most of us don't struggle to throw things away when we really need to. It's not emotionally distressing. In my own case, it's simply the fact that doing tip runs isn't high up on my to-do list when I've got more exciting mental projects on the go.

With hoarding problems, the relationship to someone's possessions is less about practicality and the useful nature of things and more about the emotional attachment and process of letting them go. But there are also other differences when compared to OCD and obsessive-compulsive personality traits.

＊ ✳ ＊

As with most problems relating to obsession and compulsion, hoarding can often start to emerge during adolescence and early adulthood. It can stem from the same range of contributory factors: early life adversity, trauma, learned beliefs, social environment, cognitive styles, and neurobiology. But it typically follows a different trajectory over time.

For example, obsessive-compulsive personality traits tend to be relatively static, consistent with broader personality patterns. With OCD, the likelihood of the onset of new symptoms tends to reduce with age. When new symptoms appear in later life, they are usually quite rare; in most cases, they tend to be associated with neurological changes such as stroke, Parkinson's disease, or dementia.[8] [9]

However, hoarding tends to become more problematic over time, with the prevalence of more significant impact tending to rise significantly in adults over the age of fifty. In fact, older adults are potentially three times more likely to experience clinically significant hoarding problems than younger people.[10] [11]

To a degree, it's also possible that the gradual accumulation of items is more likely to coincide with significant life transitions. Naturally, as we age, we face major life changes, children leaving home, bereavements, and the prospect of retirement.

The natural ageing process can also bring about cognitive changes. Our ability to categorise, remember, and make decisions can start to diminish. These processes are commonly known as *executive functions*. Although these don't necessarily directly cause hoarding, they can often exacerbate it. Someone might forget why they kept something, feel overwhelmed at the thought of organising their belongings, or struggle with deciding what to let go of.[12]

The likelihood of frailty and fractures also increases as part of the natural deterioration of the physical body. Given the nature of hoarding, which commonly involves cluttered spaces, trips and falls, fire hazards, and blocked access to essential areas of the home, it is arguably more likely to increase risk.[13]

A lot of older adults can also easily become socially isolated. Again, this is not necessarily causative but holds an increased potential to further compound the problem. Emotional attachment to objects may become more intense, particularly when experiencing the death of a spouse, having to move home, chronic illness or disability, or potentially a loss of purpose or role. This can all impact someone's sense of meaning and identity continuity.[14]

Loneliness can also have a significant impact on mental well-being more broadly, regardless of whether the person experiences compulsive behaviour or not. In both the UK and the USA, older adults face increasing levels of social disconnection, leading to depression and anxiety.[15]

People can also feel a lot of shame or stigma, which can be a barrier to seeking help. Some might avoid talking about mental health concerns altogether. At times, this might involve differences in generational attitudes around mental health problems. But there can also be systemic barriers. In the UK, despite the significant rise in mental health awareness over the past decade, older people are still less likely to be referred to mental health services than younger adults, even when their symptoms are equally severe.[16]

All sounds a bit depressing, doesn't it?

At the risk of portraying older age as all doom and gloom, it's important to remember that many older adults continue to lead full, rich, and active lives despite common physical health issues. Most of the people I know in their seventies and eighties have more active social lives than I do.

Hoarding problems can also affect people of all ages; it's simply the case that there is a higher likelihood of it becoming more problematic as we get older.

So, how do we help someone who has trouble throwing things away? This also comes with a different set of challenges.

Although treatment can and does work, one of the first issues someone might encounter is that the treatment for hoarding problems generally requires more specialist knowledge. Certainly, here in the UK, there has been a shortage of trained professionals and access to services equipped and experienced in addressing these types of issues.[17]

The most empirically supported approach is a form of cognitive-behavioural therapy. Typically, there is a focus on helping someone learn different ways of making decisions about their belongings, better understand the underlying belief system, and gradually helping them build confidence in discarding items. Often, therapy needs to be delivered in the home and at a pace that accommodates both the physical, emotional and relational factors involved.

Yet, like any psychological intervention, there has to be some degree of engagement and consent to being helped by a therapist. Sometimes, people don't realise help is available but are aware that the extent of their hoarding is causing unease and difficulty.

Naturally, there can also be a degree of avoiding seeking out help or admitting they need it for fear of revealing the extent of their problems. In some cases, a person doesn't recognise that what they are doing is a problem at all, despite threats of forced clear-ups and eviction from their property. Although less common, this is where things can get really complicated.

＊ ＊ ＊

When hoarding reaches extreme levels, such as decades of accumulation, the consequences often stretch beyond the individual person and their home. Neighbours may be affected by infestations, fire hazards, or structural risks, turning what was once a private matter into a public health and safety concern.

Ideally, local services can negotiate with the person and agree to work together to find a solution that everyone can live with. But that's not always the case. When a person doesn't consent, and the risk remains high, things can become very formal.

These situations are sometimes managed within community mental health teams or adult social care services. While I've never personally dealt with an extreme hoarding case, I've sat in many multi-agency meetings where difficult decisions had to be made. And commonly involve discussions around the person's capacity to make independent decisions.

At times, health and social care professionals can hold considerable power in someone's life. Suppose someone is significantly struggling to function or manage their environment safely In that case, it's not uncommon for their ability to make informed decisions to come into question. In England and Wales, the Mental Capacity Act (2005) provides the legal framework for assessing these types of situations.[18]

One of the most important principles in this process is the assumption that every adult can make decisions, including their right to make unwise choices. However, assessing capacity applies to specific decisions at specific times in particular contexts. A person is only considered to lack capacity if they cannot understand, retain, weigh up, or communicate the information needed to make a decision.

In practice, it's rarely straightforward.

Hoarding cases can be particularly complex. Many people are articulate, aware of their circumstances, and can clearly state that they do not want help. Yet, their ability to realistically appraise their risks, such as fire, injury, or disease from infestations, may still be significantly impaired. Emotional attachments to their possessions can override fundamental safety concerns, especially when combined with cognitive challenges or coexisting mental health conditions. At times, professionals can struggle to distinguish between stubbornness and autonomy and whether someone truly understands the consequences of their actions, including the refusal of support.[19]

Suppose a person is found to lack capacity for a specific decision, such as allowing access to their home or accepting support to clean it up. In that case, any follow-up actions must be taken in the person's best interest. This involves a structured process that weighs clinical need and objective risk against the person's known values and wishes. Family and friends should also be involved where appropriate.

As you might imagine, navigating the tension between respecting someone's rights and autonomy and preventing serious harm, not just to the individual but also potentially to others, can be really challenging. However, this still doesn't automatically grant the local authority the right to enter the person's home or begin removing their personal belongings. A best-interest decision alone does not permit forced action. Legal powers, such as court orders or statutory warrants, must still be obtained. This is part of maintaining due process and protecting individual rights, even when the risks are substantial.

Safeguarding processes can initiate coordinated action across different services, including housing, environmental health, fire safety, social care, and, if needed, emergency services. While safeguarding still does not override a person's right to make their own decisions, it provides a framework for managing serious risk through negotiation, structured support, or legal intervention where the thresholds have been met.

In most cases of hoarding, the person is likely to be deemed to have capacity and retain their legal right to make their own decisions, however hazardous those choices might be. In these cases, intervention cannot be imposed unless there's a legal basis to act. This is where environmental health teams might step in under public health legislation, such as the Environmental Protection Act (1990).[20] This allows local authority workers to issue formal notices. If these are ignored, they can seek a court order to enter the property and carry out essential works. The costs of doing so can also be reclaimed from the person.

If the property is rented, housing providers may act on tenancy breaches. This can involve written warnings, enforcement notices, or, where risks are severe, seeking eviction through the civil courts.

It's a lot of information to digest, but the bottom line is that the costs and consequences of obsessive and compulsive problems can extend well beyond the psychological well-being of the person and their relationships. Sometimes, they lead to extreme counter-measures. Yet it's important we don't lose sight of the person underneath the mental health labels, the garbage bags, or the court warrants.

* ✳ *

Mr Trebus became a public figure after the BBC documentary, and is remembered mainly by people in my age group as a quirky chap who caused chaos in North London. This was summed up in his obituary in *The Guardian*.

> "Eccentric and tenacious hoarder whose loads of rubbish brought him television fame"
> —Quoted from The Guardian, 2002.

Fair enough, the article digs deeper into his life in the main body of the text. But I would be personally mortified if that was my summary of eighty years of being in the world.

While the context surrounding the events documented by the BBC in 1999 indeed demonstrated someone who had significant difficulty discarding things, a formal psychiatric diagnosis is purely a private matter. There is no official public record of Mr Trebus having a mental health problem, and quite rightly so. Going by the video footage, I'm not entirely convinced Mr Trebus would have necessarily seen it that way, either. Nor is it for me or any other clinician to infer a diagnosis for someone we have never met.

But I would have really liked to have met him, though.

Not to wave a copy of the DSM, but to know more about him as a person. Not much is known about his life before the BBC documentary. However, there are fragmented snippets from different articles available in the public domain.

Mr Trebus was born in an area that formed part of the newly established Weimar Republic, Germany's post-imperial democratic state. The region had long been a historically contested borderland between Germany and Poland. [21]

After World War I, the Treaty of Versailles (1919) redrew many of Europe's borders. One of the aims was to re-establish a Polish state, which hadn't existed as an independent nation since the late 18th century. Large areas of land that had been part of Germany, Austria-Hungary, and Russia were ceded to the new Polish Republic.[22]

However, the border decisions were fraught with tension. In areas with mixed ethnic populations, there were armed uprisings to determine whether the territory should be part of Germany or Poland. Mr Trebus was born and raised as a German citizen, though the area had a Polish name and was predominantly Polish-speaking, typical of several regions along the eastern German-Polish border at that time.

According to *The Guardian*, his father worked as a railway station master. This role likely came with some degree of social standing. Sadly, his father died in a sudden accident, falling through weakened ice on a frozen lake. His formative years were primarily spent with his mother in the turbulent political terrain of a region caught between German and Polish rule.[23]

When World War II broke out in 1939, Mr Trebus was still living in territory that was recognised internationally as being part of Germany. This meant he was subject to German military conscription laws. Like many men in such regions, especially ethnic minorities or those from contested backgrounds, he would have had little choice but to serve in the Wehrmacht. The unified armed forces of Nazi Germany.[24]

He served until he was captured, and the accounts appear to differ slightly here. Although unverified, he was possibly taken as a prisoner of war during one of the Western European campaigns, then released or transferred and later joined the Polish Free Forces.

This would also reflect a typical pattern among many people conscripted from similar occupied regions. Once they were freed from German military service, many chose to align with the Allied forces when given the opportunity. Again, while not officially confirmed, it is believed that Mr Trebus may have joined the 1st Carpathian Anti-Tank Regiment, part of the British-commanded Polish Army, likely serving in Italy in campaigns such as Monte Cassino.[25] [26]

After the war ended, he was among thousands of Polish servicemen who faced the grim prospect of returning to a homeland now under Soviet-backed communist control. Many chose instead to remain in Britain through the Polish Resettlement Corps, fearing political persecution if they went back. According to *The Telegraph*, he married his wife, Jozefa, in 1949 and settled in North London, where they raised five children together.[27]

His neighbours recalled his sharp wit, old-world manners, and unwavering opinions, including disdain for bureaucracy and interference. His dry humour left an impression that people didn't easily forget.

According to his *Wikipedia* page, Mr Trebus was also an avid collector and admirer of Elvis Presley, owning nearly every record he released. He also enjoyed mechanical repairs, particularly vacuum cleaners, which he collected, dismantled, and restored with care.[28]

His obituary in *The Guardian* states that he separated from his wife in 1981; his children had already flown the nest, and the routines of family life may have given way to increased solitude.

Yet, he still interacted with neighbours, engaged in debates with passers-by, and stood firmly by his right to live as he chose.

During his later years, his living conditions deteriorated, drawing the attention of the local authorities. Ultimately, mounting health concerns and external pressure led to his eventual relocation to Trentfield Nursing Home in Southgate, where he spent the final days of his long life.[29]

Mr Trebus died in September 2002, a couple of months before his 84th birthday. He was a son, a veteran, a husband and father, a fixer of hoovers, and a devoted fan of Elvis Presley. His story is undoubtedly one of eclecticism but also one of endurance and identity.

I just hope that if I manage to live into my eighties, workaholism and my peculiar habits will not be the standout headlines of my own eclectic life.

13

Drawing Circles

To live in hearts we leave behind is not to die
—Thomas Campbell

O ften, the greatest fear isn't death. It's being forgotten.

Many of us have a complicated relationship with the concept of loss, despite it being one of the few certainties that we all share. My own perspective and exposure to death have shifted considerably since clinical training. Life experience and maturation also likely helped. It would certainly be hard for me to believe during my twenties that I would help people process complex bereavement. However, loss appears across many themes in therapy. Grief is not just experienced in the context of mortality but also in the form of missed opportunities, the end of relationships, unfulfilled roles, the absence of play, care and emotional nurture during childhood.

But there is a discomfort that comes with the concept of mortality, that life is finite and uncontrollable. While most people have an awareness of death, many haven't necessarily adapted to the idea of it. Sometimes, this is through limited exposure when they are young. It's very common for parents to want to protect their children from feeling sad or upset. Still, it can sometimes be a bit clunky.

Most children, particularly in Western cultures, first encounter death through the loss of a pet. It's not uncommon to wake up to find a goldfish floating in the bowl one morning. A rabbit cage left open and empty. While these moments are early opportunities to learn about mortality in developmentally honest ways, there is often a temptation to sanitise it. "Bobby the bunny ran away." "The dog left to live on a farm." "We'll get another fish." "Grandma has gone to heaven; she's happy, though. Don't be sad—here's a Ninja Turtle; now grab your bag for school."

It's often well-meant and done to protect a young mind from suffering distress. At times, it's simply about perceiving that the child is too young to understand or grasp the concept. But it can also skew the truth and sometimes delay emotional and cognitive processing surrounding the event. How a child is told about the death of a close family member, in particular, can lead to complicated grief and internal states of distress.[1] This can also impact their emotional development well into adulthood.

Children as young as five can begin to understand the idea of death if given the chance to explore it in age-appropriate ways. Suppose the explanation is vague, minimised, or withheld altogether. It may leave a child confused and lead to them developing distorted or incomplete beliefs around it.[2]

I'm speaking here as a clinician, not as a parent. My job is much easier, but I do spend many hours of the week rummaging around childhood memories. Parents commonly struggle with loss themselves, avoiding or blocking it. At times, they can unintentionally project their own anxieties onto their children. Potentially replicating their own upbringing. But it's still important to help a child understand death as a realistic and natural part of life. If you kick the can down the road with your ten-year-old right now, they may be telling their therapist about it in twenty years.

I'm not suggesting that the topic should be forced onto a young person; instead, it's about allowing space when questions arise. Using clear language. Being there for emotional support. Letting them know you are there if they need you. Acknowledging sadness without rushing in to try to fix it or immediately patch things up. It takes time.

In clinical practice, anxiety around death crops up a lot, mostly it's indirect or implicit. It often underpins health anxiety or preventative compulsions around causing serious harm. Stuck and complicated grief is also commonly experienced within the context of persisting symptoms of depression in adults, sometimes termed *melancholic* or *pathological mourning*.[3]

With perfectionism and demanding internal standards, it's more often a sense of running out of time. It's just not entirely clear what we're hell-bent on running towards, or from, or why we're even running at all.

Freud viewed death anxiety as being central to the human condition. At a deeper unconscious level, we struggle to conceive of the idea of our own extinction. Instead, we consciously preoccupy ourselves with less threatening anxieties, such as worrying about unlikely scenarios or outcomes, rather than directly facing the potential of loss, punishment, or *annihilation of the self*.[4]

But it can be costly.

When we try to avoid or outrun loss, we end up living in our heads, consumed by distractions. For some, they become immersed and hyper-focused on specific areas of life rather than actually being present in it.

The drive for achievement, legacy-building, and status can easily become prioritised over intimacy or meaning-making. Reputation over relationship. The philosopher Ernest Becker described this tendency as our *hero system*. This is a psychological defence against the *terror of our own impermanence*.[5]

Existentialist thinkers, such as Martin Heidegger, viewed loss as a defining feature of being human. As *beings toward death*, we are the only known species on earth that are uniquely aware of our own ending in advance.[6] From this perspective, death might be viewed as an invitation to live our lives with purpose and intention.

It's a lot to think about, isn't it?

If you struggle with excessive worry around death, you're not on your own. It took me a long time to get my head around it. During my late teens, I quite fancied the idea of being a vampire. I mean, I couldn't stand the thought of drinking blood and killing things. But immortality as a vegetarian felt like a reasonable compromise.

During my mid-twenties, I attended my first funeral. I really didn't want to go, but a friend was going as well, and I didn't want to let them down. I managed to get to the church by distracting myself right up until the point that the coffin was being brought down the aisle.

Unfortunately, by that point, the reality suddenly kicked in, and I wasn't prepared for it. My nervous system couldn't cope, and I started with an uncontrollable fit of nervous laughter. The worst kind, though. The type where the context is highly inappropriate. Other people may begin to think you're a sociopath, and that just makes it worse.

I managed to bury my face in a hymn sheet, and someone placed a hand on my back, thinking I was sobbing, noticing my shoulders bouncing up and down. Safe to say, it wasn't the proudest moment of my life, and I felt terrible about it for weeks. I also made a lot of excuses to avoid funerals for several years after, fearing it would happen again.

"So sorry, I can't get the time off work."

That changed over time through natural exposure, and it turned out that none of my experiences ever matched the degree of anxiety I had built them up to be. I've also encountered circumstances that I never even thought about.

+ ✳ +

My friend Hollie is a career worrier and has lived with multiple physical health issues from a young age. While I've always focused on work at the expense of everything else, Hollie tends to focus on everyone else at the expense of herself. With a full-time job and caring responsibilities, she rarely stops to draw breath, let alone rest. Until something gave way in 2017—the electrical activity in her heart.

She'd gone to work that morning as usual. Feeling unwell was normal for her, but this time was different. She carried on stoically, brushing it off despite experiencing what she described as "funny turns" at the office. One afternoon, she felt so unwell that she went home. That evening, her partner, Bruno, called an ambulance.

Many anxious hours later, a captioned photo appeared on my phone. Her neck was fitted with a cannula with lots of tubes sticking out of it. "Well, James. I've been both shocked and am in shock." What she didn't mention until I arrived during visiting hours was that she'd nearly died.

Resuscitated twice.

The NHS team had worked intensively to stabilise her. The "funny turns" had been a rare cardiovascular event, made more complicated by unexpected news. After years of believing she couldn't conceive, she was pregnant with "Squiggle," her actual name in utero. It was only the start of a long road.

The pregnancy was at higher risk. She was hospitalised again with another dangerous, life-threatening condition. By chance, the hospital was located in the same city where I worked, so I visited regularly after finishing my clinic.

At only twenty-four weeks into the pregnancy, the scans were showing the baby had stopped growing, and her vital signs were quickly deteriorating. The team were preparing for delivery, believing there was little hope. Without urgent intervention, the risk was that neither of them would survive.

And still—there was a heartbeat.

A tiny one. Belonging to Squiggle, who made her dramatic debut into the world and was placed in an incubator in the neonatal intensive care unit, kicking her legs underneath special lights. Alarms going off every two minutes.

NICU is unlike any place I've ever experienced. It's a space where life begins under intensive monitoring, and the line between fear and hope can sometimes feel paper-thin. The NHS team were extraordinary, with many skilled and determined nurses. But they're working with the most fragile of human lives. Nothing is guaranteed. Most babies do survive, but it's a rollercoaster.

New parents often find themselves facing the heartbreaking task of beginning to bond while preparing to say goodbye at the same time.

Squiggle had been doing okay, but the pain on Hollie and Bruno's faces was unmistakable. We were all sitting beside the incubator, watching her sleep. My mind wandered to thinking about what my own parents might have felt, watching me through the same Plexiglass.

But mostly, I was transfixed. She looked like a tiny purple baby bird, perfectly formed but incredibly delicate. Her hand curled around my little finger as I reached into the incubator. She wasn't even my child, yet I felt the warm spread of love in my chest instantly. The natural human bonding process was already in the post.

Then the alarms went off—again.

This time, something was clearly different. The nurses moved faster. Their faces more focused and concerned. Squiggle was suddenly deteriorating. The ward team began helping Hollie and Bruno prepare for the worst.

They were encouraged to make footprints of her feet on card with non-toxic ink. I couldn't begin to imagine what they were feeling. Admittedly, I considered leaving. Partly out of respect, not wanting to intrude. The other part was an urge to avoid witnessing what might be coming next. The arrival of the hospital chaplain hit me hard. Hollie and Bruno looked frozen to the spot.

It was very surreal.

When I left the office at 5 pm, I hadn't expected being asked to be Squiggle's godparent and attend her Christening by 8 pm. Time seemed to have been suspended. A grief-filled void between love and loss. Still, the importance of presence, care, and remembering, despite the chaos and anxiety.

But somehow, she pulled through. Again. And again.

There were months of turbulence ahead on the neonatal ward, followed by physical and neurological challenges that she has since taken mostly in her stride. Today, she's a headstrong, endlessly busy eight-year-old living life to its fullest.

It was a harrowing time for the family. But it was also a privilege to be part of their experience.

Grief, like all other emotions, has an important function. It is the body's natural, neurobiological response to loss. But many people struggle with it.

Lois Tonkin's grief model is commonly used in bereavement settings to explain why the pain of loss doesn't necessarily disappear with time.[7] It has been widely adapted for use across various contexts and offers a simple yet powerful visual.

Imagine two circles, both the same size. These represent the difficulty—in this case, the pain of grief. The first is tightly enclosed by a box, symbolising life immediately after the loss, where everything is consumed by it. The second box is larger. It represents the return to daily life: ordinary routines, new experiences, the gradual re-expansion of a life that can once again contain joy. The concept is that grief doesn't shrink, but life grows around it. It becomes integrated rather than erased. Less dominant. It can be a comforting idea.

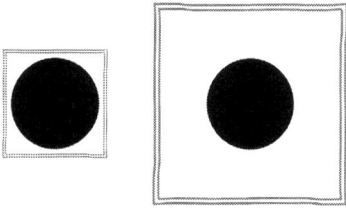

Adapted from Tonkin (1996)

But it has limits, especially after traumatic bereavement. People may try to grey out the circle entirely. The fear of facing the enormity of the loss can trigger a defensive response. The fear of moving on, forgetting, or closing a door. Paradoxically, this often results in forgetting and closing off.

When grief remains stuck in an unacceptable or terrorised state, for example, when the nervous system cannot metabolise it, this often leads to prolonged distress. What may seem strange is that it can actually inhibit remembering. Positive memories get blocked as the body's natural healing process stalls.

But we actually need death to live. We often talk about it as something separate from life. A rare, isolated event we only confront occasionally. Especially when we're young, we often imagine it as distant and abstract. In adulthood, we tend to avoid thinking about it. Pushing it to the back of our mind.

But you can't experience loss without there first being life. And you can't have real life without the possibility of love. Which means the price of love is the risk of loss. One doesn't happen without the other. Nor can we feel the pain of loss without having first experienced connection. They come as a package deal, no matter how much we try to surgically separate or categorise them.

And when we apply this to obsession and compulsion, it isn't just the intense focus on the weird, intrusive images or career aspirations sitting at the surface of the problem that causes the main difficulty. It's the over-engagement with the things we do to avoid facing what lies beneath. The rituals. The checking. The rigid control. All of it can function, consciously or otherwise, as a strategy to avoid grief. Or fear. Or the unbearable awareness that nothing in life is truly certain—other than death.

This doesn't mean people with obsessive-compulsive tendencies are incapable of feeling love, grief, or connection. On the contrary, many are exceptionally capable. But their attention and cognitive energy are often pulled away, distracted from the emotional centre of things once anxiety takes hold. Still, allowing ourselves to engage fully with love means opening ourselves to loss. To live in the present means we must surrender control over excessive attempts to control our safety. And to grieve is to acknowledge that nothing in the past can be undone, only remembered.

So what happens when our own hands of time come close to striking midnight? Do we suddenly start ramping up the final checks of electrical sockets, or give those work emails a final scan with a fine-tooth comb before we sign off, allowing our minds to finally settle?

Job done! No regrets?

It would appear not.

———— * ✳ * ————

Regret is often dismissed as wasted energy, a form of useless hindsight or self-indulgent rumination. Cognitive models of therapy sometimes cast it as a faulty mental loop, best redirected or reframed. But regret is important, provided we use the perspectives generated from it wisely.

It's a complex state that straddles both emotion and cognition, tied to agency, memory, and meaning. It arises when we recognise that a different choice, one we were capable of making, might have led to a better outcome.

Unlike guilt, which implies wrongdoing, regret doesn't necessarily involve remorse. It is more often a recognition of absence or of missed potential. Yet the two are connected. Regret, when not defended against or prematurely bypassed, can stir the imagination. It may awaken a desire to repair, reconnect, or live differently in the future. It also commonly appears in the context of grief and loss.

Rather than being a flaw in our thinking, it can form part of our experiences that actually keep us tethered to a more fulfilled life, even at the end of it.

An extensive study published in 2000 surveyed over four hundred patients, families, and healthcare providers to identify what matters most at the end of life.[8] The highest-rated priorities were not legacy, achievement, or goal completion. They were pain relief, emotional support, mental awareness, and the presence of loved ones.

This was also supported by the accounts from palliative care practitioners. Bronnie Ware, a former palliative care nurse, documented recurring themes during end-of-life discussions.[9] Common regrets included not living a life true to oneself, working too hard, not staying in touch with friends, and not allowing oneself to be happier during times of good health.

The themes lean toward the idea that unease and distress at the end of life often centre on lost time, missed relationships, and being unnecessarily emotionally restrained.

More recent studies point to marked experiences of people with obsessive-compulsive traits. A systematic review published in 2023 found that those with elevated obsessive traits had reported significantly higher levels of existential dissatisfaction and depressive symptoms near the end of their life.[10]

However, these were not short-term mood states related to adjustment; they were persistent feelings of disappointment in how their lives had actually been lived. Mainly, the reported distress was around the degree of rigidity and excessive control they held over themselves and the perceived failure to prioritise intimacy and closeness.

Traits such as orderliness, conscientiousness, and moral responsibility can support general functioning during the summer and autumn of life. But they appear to offer less protection in the final stages of winter, particularly when emotional flexibility and connection become more central.

* ✳ *

No one can reliably predict the day their life will end. The time any of us has remaining will vary depending on age, health, and countless unknown factors. But imagine, for a moment, if you can bear it, that you're on the final day of your life. It may be challenging to go there, but try. What will be on your shelf of marvellous things?

The top shelf is where the most notable achievements tend to reside. Career milestones and qualifications. Recognition. Eight million views on your YouTube Channel. A fancy job title. Luxury cars. You've likely put a lot of effort into getting them, whatever they are. And they may still feel important. But here's the question: would you trade any of them to get more time back? If so, what would you exchange it for?

And then there's the bottom shelf of *useless things*. This is full of the stuff that we dismissed or ignored, filed away under lock and key. Rubbish, pointless, poorly performing, bad and terrible stuff. Perhaps your last therapist is sitting in there. This book is potentially en route. But if you looked closely? Any pieces of advice, relationships, confrontations, or "growth opportunities" that might have been of use?

Which shelf will matter the most? What things would you most want to be remembered for? Why is that?

Don't get me wrong. I'm not suggesting that you would want to live life focusing only on regrets. But we can use regret to spur reflection to inform our future needs, right here and now. When held in balance, it may help better leverage opportunities for the time ahead.

And we will each have our needs and things that we value. Life would be incredibly dull if we were all the same. The aim is to promote realistic well-being, not to impose prescribed wellness activities. My own career sits firmly on the top of my shelf of marvellous things, and it would likely stay there. Not because I idealise it, but because it reflects reality. It has shaped a significant part of how I perceive myself, not only through clinical work, but also through the perspectives and understanding it has provided me. But it's not my whole story.

Are there things I would do differently given the chance again? Sure! But I can't change time. Not what's already gone. What may sound strange is that I would hesitate to go back to my childhood to fix health anxiety and OCD. Granted, it would have brought relief at the time. But my life may have taken a different course. I doubt I would be in the job I'm in now, and I have met many good friends through the process. I wouldn't want to trade that.

What I do have available to me now is knowledge about myself. That was also gained through circumstances driven by difficulty. That now comes with the awareness that I have the choice to change what I do. Not to avoid the possibility of future regret, but to prepare myself for the inevitable transitions that lie ahead. One of those is retirement.

I understand myself well enough by now to know that I am likely to struggle with that in around twenty years, unless I begin the process of adjusting to the idea of it now.

Why?

If you've ever watched a sprint runner cross the finish line, you'll know they don't simply stop the second their race ends. The momentum that is built carries them forward. They don't suddenly start slowing down as they approach the line. But if there isn't much track left beyond that, they end up hurtling into the barriers or crash mats.

So, I'm preparing for that crash now. Very gradually slowing the pace before the finish line. Giving my younger parts the space to breathe. Intentionally doing things I've wanted to do but have been putting off. This book is part of that. Balancing out seriousness and routine with more creativity and play. Pushing back against the professional critic in the attic of my mind.

It's not easy, nor am I *brilliant* at it. But if I don't try, the building team at work will likely have to pry my fingers from my office door, one by one, when the time eventually comes to hand back the keys. I also want to add valuable experiences to my memory bank while I still can.

As we head into the final chapter, I'm inviting you once again to travel back in time for one final rummage through my childhood experiences.

This time, it's a very different kind of story.

But an important one.

14

Leveraging Life

We must consider that great responsibility follows inseparably from great power

—Voltaire

W hy don't you follow your dreams?

If only it were that easy. There can be a lot in the way. When it comes to living life more fully, with intention, many of us have already set about trying to stack the odds in our favour. In most cases, we try to control external things. But we often miss a vital component. This was the case for a troubled young boy in *The NeverEnding Story* (1984).[1] My sister and I were both completely obsessed with it, and it was compulsive viewing in our house growing up. Although it's a children's film, it's psychologically rich, offering some highly relevant lessons when viewed from an adult perspective.

The main protagonist is Bastian, a shy bookworm who has been having a difficult time. He's being bullied at school, and his grades are slipping.

On his way to class, he encounters a group of kids who start chasing him, and he locks himself in the school attic with a mysterious book. He begins to follow the journey of Atreyu, a young warrior tasked with saving the land of *Fantasia* from a destructive force known only as *The Nothing*.

Bastian doesn't realise how central he is to the fight against destruction, and that the boundaries between the reader and the story aren't quite as fixed as they first appear. It was a staple classic of the 80s and has stood the test of time for decades.

I could relate to Bastian a lot, though. He was sensitive and imaginative, but also socially withdrawn. He would often escape into fantasy rather than confronting the reality around him. I equally spent a lot of time hiding away with a book myself.

Like most children, I viewed it through a young lens and didn't fully grasp the deeper conceptual meaning behind it all. But it gave me my first exposure to the awareness of death. The image of Atreyu's beloved horse, Artax, sinking into the mud of the *Swamp of Sadness* is still burned into my hippocampus. No doubt it traumatised generations to come.

My little sister would have been about five at the time, getting her age-appropriate introduction to loss. Naturally, we came from a household of animal lovers, and I was absolutely mortified about Artax, but I was mostly just cross. I simply couldn't understand why Atreyu would risk taking his horse into a swamp in the first place. I was preempting Artax sinking before it even happened. "He probably weighs more than my Dad's Sierra. What the hell are you thinking!"

Obviously, if you're in a rush to find the answer to the end of the world, you're counting on strength and speed. But sadly, Atreyu was now going it alone on foot. He pushes forward no matter the cost, always focused on the mission, often ignoring his own limits.

But his character was the one that I actually struggled to relate to the most, at the time. While many children idealised him, I was already an overly cautious kid and wasn't so keen on him. I thought he was too cocky. He reminded me of a boy at school whom I had tried to befriend. Unfortunately, he just pretended to be my friend, making comments behind my back.

One day, he tripped me up in the school dining hall. Everyone laughed. Which was bad enough, but I'd also dropped my raspberry sponge pudding with school custard. It was my favourite. We only got it once a week. That was the final straw!

In the opening scenes of the film, the bookstore owner told Bastian that the best way to deal with a bully was to give them "a good punch on the nose". So I did! Raspberry sauce still on my hand for dramatic effect. It just made things worse and got me into a lot of trouble. My parents were called into school. I wasn't going to be doing that again! So I remained on the periphery instead.

———— * ✳ * ————

When Atreyu met *Morla, the Ancient One,* I started to warm to him a bit more. Morla was a cranky old giant turtle, living in complete isolation in the swamp. Dismissive and uninterested, just sneezing and complaining all the time. My sister thought she was hilarious. I couldn't stand her, though. She reminded me of one of my junior school teachers.

Sally, my friend, was really good at maths and always got lots of praise from the teacher. She even gave her extra time for homework if she needed it. "Oh, Sally, your handwriting is beautiful, so neat," she would say, while showing her work to the whole class in morning assembly.

But I was rubbish at maths, I couldn't spell, and my handwriting looked like a spider had crawled over it. I would regularly stand by the teacher's desk, smiling politely, hoping for some help. Still, no luck. She would just blow her nose without looking up. "You need to try harder. Everything you need is in your book." I stopped asking after that. Not wanting to be told off again. So I would draw shapes instead.

But she did teach me a lesson. One afternoon, she took my paper, full of doodles, off my desk and showed it to the entire class, just as she had with Sally.

"Can anyone tell me what type of maths this is?"

I was instantly embarrassed, shot out of my seat and grabbed the paper from her hand, ripping it up.

"You RUDE boy!" she shouted, as she poked me in the chest. Giggles echoed around the classroom.

Atreyu didn't get much help either. Morla's advice? "You might as well not bother!" The answer he needed was at *The Southern Oracle*, but it was too far away, and probably not worth the effort. The resigned pessimism just baffled me. "Why can't she just admit that she doesn't want to help him? At least he would know where he stood!" Atreyu wasn't fazed by it, though; he just trudged on through the mud regardless.

* ✳ *

There was one particular scene in the film that really unnerved me. A pair of ancient statues that could vaporise you if you weren't confident enough. There was no way I would be running through that! I'd have been zapped to dust by a laser beam. But I was willing for Atreyu to believe in himself and keep going. Bastian was as well.

But *The Mirror Gate* threw me. Atreyu sees his own reflection at first, but then the image distorts—suddenly, it's Bastian looking back. I didn't really get it at the time. I thought it was a magic portal. The entire plot was beginning to converge on the merging of two worlds.

By this point, Fantasia was crumbling with rocks flying everywhere. Bastian was still reading on in denial, and I was glad. "It's a death trap, just stay in the attic, nice and safe with your book!" I would have probably just closed the cover and taken it back to the shop at that point. "This item appears to have a fault. Not as expected!"

Besides, there was still *Gmork* to come. He was a big wolf lurking in the shadows—a messenger for *The Nothing*. My sister was terrified of him.

When I was a kid, I thought Gmork was meant to be some kind of demon. However, the storyline wasn't a fight between good and evil, unlike most films of that era. *The Nothing* was actually a nihilistic force driven by the loss of imagination and the erosion of self-belief. Naturally, it's a big concept to get your head around when you're nine.

But it turned out that Bastian, the central character, was both the biggest threat to Fantasia and also its saviour. He just needed to start seeing himself as being important enough to matter to his own story.

In the climactic scene of the film, the Empress of Fantasia makes a final plea to Bastian to take action. "Why don't you follow your dreams?"

He eventually wakes from his denial and starts the process of rebuilding things from just a single grain of sand.

His first task was straightforward.

He needs to make his first wish.

Although I resonated with Bastian the most, my favourite character in the entire film was always Falkor. He was a huge luck dragon that always arrived just in the nick of time. He saved Atreyu's bacon on more than one occasion. He reminded me of our dog Jamie. He had the same daft grin on his face with a fluffy beard. Jamie would always spin around the house, wagging his tail when I got home from school to cheer me up.

I used to imagine flying around the streets of Wakefield on Falkor's back, much like Bastian in the film's final scene. He terrified the school bullies to the point that they threw themselves into an industrial-sized bin of terrible things. It would have solved a lot of problems for me at the time, especially if I could get Mrs Bolton to jump in there as well.

But the film goes much deeper than many of us were consciously aware of as young people.

In fact, the entire arc of the film takes us straight into the core of what underpins most psychological problems, including obsession and compulsion.

Our inner emotional management.

On the one hand, we could view the film as a simple fantasy adventure. The story of a young boy bridging two separate worlds, reality and imagination. Naturally, that's how we understood it as children. But when viewed through a psychological lens, it represents only one world. The main characters and events in Fantasia are not separate from Bastian—they *are* Bastian.

The opening scenes depict a young person already living inside a dissociated part of himself. He is managing fear and sadness through avoidance and is already learning to run and hide from the challenges of life.

From the moment he opens *The NeverEnding Story*, we're immediately inside his emotional world, or, in psychological-speak, his Internal Family System (IFS).

✦ ✦ ✦

Richard C. Schwartz developed the concept of IFS.[2] It's a way of helping people understand complex emotional processes by viewing the mind as distinct *parts*. Each part has different roles or patterns of feeling and behaviour that serve a particular protective function.

These are not "symptoms" or flaws in our personality They're often early adaptive responses that continue to operate in the background, even when they're no longer helpful. In IFS, these parts are grouped into three main types: Managers, Exiles, and Firefighters.

Managers are typically the more proactive parts. Their role is to prevent us from feeling emotional discomfort, such as shame, humiliation, or helplessness, by keeping external life in order. These are the parts that drive us to organise excessively, stick rigidly to routines, manage relationships tightly, aim for perfection, or take on too much responsibility. They are often experienced as inner critics, over-functioning achievers, or excessively keen strategists.

Exiles, by contrast, are the parts that carry emotional pain. They often hold early experiences of vulnerability, powerlessness, or the belief that we are unimportant, unlovable, or unsafe. Because these emotions can be overwhelming, the system usually pushes Exiles out of view. But they don't disappear. They remain active beneath the surface and become threatened by things that echo earlier experiences.

Firefighters are more reactive protectors. Their job is to jump in quickly when an Exile is scared, using whatever strategy they can to shut down the emotional intensity. This might include distraction, impulsive behaviour, substance use, or avoidance. In more extreme cases, especially in people with trauma histories, Firefighters may use dissociation to shut the system down entirely. These strategies are often intense because their primary aim is to provide immediate relief. That can include strong defensive reactions, passive-aggressive behaviour, or verbal attack—anything that stops it dead in its tracks.

Underpinning all of these parts is what IFS refers to as the *Self*. This is not a part, but a core state characterised by calm, clarity, and curiosity. I think of it as a kind of internal equilibrium. When we are in Self, we're able to observe our parts without being overwhelmed by them. We can listen to them, understand them, and respond with leadership rather than urgency or avoidance.

The aim is not to eliminate parts. It's to help the system become more integrated, so that each part can do their jobs in ways that genuinely serve us. This is what *Self-leadership* means. It's about having enough internal space and stability to guide our system with greater awareness, rather than being driven by old patterns or becoming overly emotionally reactive.[3]

With more internal coordination, we're better able to leverage opportunities to live life, rather than constantly feeling stuck in survival mode, firefighting, over-managing, or trying to outrun discomfort.

Granted, we didn't build the system on our own, but we do have full authority to go in and update the program. Not to increase the control, but as a steady process of letting go of what is familiar. That makes tangible long-term change possible.

The challenge is that the adult *Self* is often buried under years of early blended roles and protective strategies that have been operating in isolation.

Again, integration isn't a specific ideal that we must reach, or attempt to manufacture ourselves into someone that we do not recognise, or try to live how we would not wish to be. We also each have different variations of our internal world.

* ✳ *

If this all sounds a tad vague, test it out. Right now.

Pay attention to your body. What do you notice?

What's the general vibe? Your thoughts and feelings?

If you're calm, curious, or rational, that's your *Self*.

But if you're similar to how I was during my earlier attempts at therapy, perhaps you're quick to dismiss. "It sounds shit. Not interested!" Is it possible that *Morla, the Ancient One,* might be sneezing away in an isolated space in your mind? Is there anyone in your life who modelled that to you?

You might experience a more nihilistic outlook. "It's all pointless. Nothing changes. None of this matters!" One of your Firefighters may be similar to *Gmork*. Not necessarily angry or with bad intentions, but a part that immediately tries to shut down the entire system to avoid feeling disappointed. This can lead to existential paralysis, blocking creativity, imagination, and self-belief—*The Nothing*.

When did you learn that was a helpful thing to do? Did it protect you at one point? Is it still needed? If so, why is that?

In simple terms, people with OCD are often dominated by Firefighters and anxious Managers. The Firefighters want to shut down distress quickly, with urgent compulsions—whatever it takes to bring swift relief. Sometimes the Managers try to keep everything under control to an excess, so that nothing goes wrong in the first place. Both are trying to protect Exiles who carry strong feelings.

With OCPD, it's typically the Managers who dominate. These parts focus on order, standards, and structure. Their job is to prevent criticism, failure, or rejection at all costs by keeping the system very tightly in line. Constantly monitoring for cracks. There are usually fewer Firefighters, but the system can be just as burdened, especially if something threatens to disrupt the rules they're working so hard to enforce.

In both cases, the system is doing its best to function, but is doing so without support from a more integrated system.

For that, you might need Falkor, a more hopeful Manager part, whose job is to keep the system moving, maintain hope, and support self-advocacy. Helping you stand up to the bullies or tormentors renting space in your head for free.

Falkor's strategy is gentle forward motion, appearing just in time and disappearing when not needed. This is characteristic of a high-functioning protector part. Imagine what it would be like if you had a fifty-foot pearlescent dragon closing your laptop when you're stuck in those work emails, or catching you when you're sinking in the swamp of self-diagnosis, up to your neck in the umpteenth fantastical ailment, or imagined prison sentence.

So, what happens if you're already feeling fired up and motivated in warrior mode? "This psychotherapy business sounds like the cure! Where do I sign up?!" Then, your inner Atreyu might already be preparing to gallop ahead to find the answers, provided you can find the *correct* answers.

But that can often be similar to the quest of reaching the Southern Oracle.

* ✳ *

In fact, the primary sequence of events in the film isn't far off the process of psychotherapy, regardless of the type of therapy you may be doing.

The scientist that Falkor brings Atreyu to see plays a similar role to that of a psychotherapist. He can offer guidance about what lies ahead, as well as support and knowledge about how he might approach different tasks. However, he plays a minor role in the grand scheme of things. He can't complete the journey on Atreyu's behalf. It's Atreyu himself who has to walk through.

The first task involves allowing yourself to be truly seen. For many people, especially those carrying shame-based defences, this can feel threatening. Vulnerability brings the fear of being exposed, judged, or even annihilated.

Things can also get harder. The therapist's role is also to help you face yourself in a metaphorical mirror—to see more clearly what you do, why you do it, and how it affects your system. Sometimes, the reflection is disorienting. It can mobilise complex feelings and impulses. Not everyone likes what they see.

And then, we reach the Southern Oracle itself. There are likely answers, but they're not always simple. Sometimes, what we hear or realise feels unreachable or beyond our current capacity. Therapy rarely offers neat solutions. Often, it leads to more questions that take time to work through.

But better integration means that our internal parts no longer need to operate in isolation or remain locked in defensive states. It creates a more stable internal environment where different emotions, impulses, and perspectives can be acknowledged and managed more effectively in collaboration.

The more trust you develop with your *Self*, the more options become available. Attention is no longer consumed by urgent internal negotiations. We have more energy available to focus on other things. Maybe even take a week off—but without finishing unpaid work, replying to Sandra from admin, or rehearsing everything that could go wrong.

Giving the internal system a well-deserved rest.

Make decisions based not only on fear or internal demands, but on genuine interests, values, and desires.

This doesn't mean dismantling the whole system. Many of our parts are useful. But we can't know which ones are truly helping unless we're in touch with them. In practical terms, this means pausing long enough to ask: "Why am I doing this?" and "What am I afraid will happen if I stop?"

Still, with enough patience and internal permission, things can start to shift. As the protective parts begin to trust that they no longer have to do everything alone, the system becomes less fragmented. Different parts start to cooperate.

And with growing awareness and self-agency, we can initiate a steady process of restoration, building upon what already exists. For some, that may be a small grain of sand.

But even with a single grain, there's hope.

Next, it requires you to give yourself permission to do something purely in your best interest. These may not be tasks that feel easy.

They also need to be things that are within your power to change. Even if that requires a bit of help and support.

All of your internal parts are important, but it also means that you need to see yourself as being important enough, too.

So, why don't you follow your dreams?

What would be your first wish?

* ✳ *

Before you go....

I really hope that you enjoyed the book.

If it so happens that this may be heading for your shelf of marvellous things, please consider leaving a review.

It makes a bigger difference than you might think.

Reviews help other readers find the book, and they play a huge role in the success and visibility of independently published work. Even a short, honest comment is incredibly valuable and very much appreciated.

Many thanks again for your time spent reading my ramblings.

Try to take care.

James

Endnotes

Checking Boxes

1. American Psychiatric Association. (2013). *Diagnostic and statistical manual of mental disorders* (5th ed.). Arlington, VA: American Psychiatric Publishing.

2. Hezel, D. M., & Simpson, H. B. (2019). Exposure and response prevention for obsessive–compulsive disorder: A review and new directions. *Journal of Clinical Psychology, 75*(1), 1–25.

3. Williams, M. T., Farris, S. G., Turkheimer, E., & Pinto, A. (2011). Symptom dimensions in obsessive–compulsive disorder: Phenomenology and treatment outcomes with exposure and ritual prevention. *Psychopathology, 44*(2), 81–89.

4. Freud, S. (1959). *Character and anal erotism*. In J. Strachey (Ed. & Trans.), *The standard edition of the complete psychological works of Sigmund Freud* (Vol. 9, pp. 169–175). London: Hogarth Press. (Original work published 1908)

5. American Psychiatric Association. (2022). *Diagnostic and statistical manual of mental disorders* (5th ed., text rev.). American Psychiatric Publishing.

6. Frost, R. O., Marten, P., Lahart, C., & Rosenblate, R. (1990). The dimensions of perfectionism. *Cognitive Therapy and Research,* 14(5), 449–468.

7. Egan, S. J., Wade, T. D., & Shafran, R. (2011). Perfectionism as a transdiagnostic process: A clinical review. *Clinical Psychology Review,* 31(2), 203–212.

8. Gros, D. F., Szafranski, D. D., Mims, B. A., & Morland, L. A. (2022). A systematic review and meta-analysis of exposure therapy outcomes for obsessive-compulsive disorder. *Journal of Anxiety Disorders.*

9. Ferrando, S. J., Wachtel, L. E., & Martino, D. J. (2023). Advances in obsessive-compulsive disorder treatment: Current strategies and emerging approaches. *Current Psychiatry Reports*, 25(1), 45–56.

10. Futh, A., Simonds, L. M., & Schaefer, J. D. (2022). Outcomes of psychological therapies for obsessive-compulsive disorder in children and adolescents: A systematic review and meta-analysis. *Clinical Child and Family Psychology Review*, 25(1), 1–19.

11. Torres, A. R., Prince, M. J., Bebbington, P., Bhugra, D., Brugha, T. S., Farrell, M., ... & Singleton, N. (2020). Obsessive-compulsive disorder and suicide risk: Results from the British National Psychiatric Morbidity Survey. *Journal of Affective Disorders*, 260, 724–729.

12. Fineberg, N. A., Hollander, E., Pallanti, S., Walitza, S., Grünblatt, E., Dell'Osso, B., ... & Stein, D. J. (2020). Clinical advances in obsessive-compulsive disorder: A position statement by the International College of Obsessive-Compulsive Spectrum Disorders. *International Clinical Psychopharmacology*, 35(4), 173–193.

13. Waller, G., & Turner, H. (2016). Therapist drift redux: Why well-meaning clinicians fail to deliver evidence-based therapy, and how to get back on track. *Behaviour Research and Therapy*, 77, 129–137.

14. Glazier, K., Swing, M., McGinn, L. K., & Abramowitz, J. S. (2015). The role of perceived stigma and self-concealment in treatment-seeking attitudes and internalizing symptoms. *The Journal of Clinical Psychiatry, 76*(6), 774–780.

15. Antshel, K. M., & Russo, N. (2019). Autism spectrum disorders and ADHD: Overlapping phenomenology, diagnostic issues, and treatment considerations. *Current Psychiatry Reports, 21*(5), 34.

16. van den Berg, D. P. G., van Os, J., Vermeiren, R. R. J. M., & van der Gaag, M. (2024). Comorbidity of OCD and neurodevelopmental disorders: Towards a developmental psychopathology model. *Biological Psychiatry*, 95(4), 298–307.

17. Thapar, A., & Cooper, M. (2016). Attention deficit hyperactivity disorder. *The Lancet, 387*(10024), 1240–1250.

18. Livingston, L. A., Shah, P., & Happé, F. (2019). Compensatory strategies below the behavioural surface in autism: A qualitative study. *The Lancet Psychiatry*, *6*(9), 766–777.

19. American Psychiatric Association. (2013). *Diagnostic and statistical manual of mental disorders* (5th ed.). Arlington, VA: American Psychiatric Publishing.

20. Lopez, C., Michelini, G., Riglin, L., & Thapar, A. (2024). The co-occurrence of ADHD and internalising problems: A developmental perspective. *Journal of Affective Disorders*, *344*, 329–340.

21. Crane, L., Adams, F., Harper, G., Welch, J., & Pellicano, E. (2021). 'Something needs to change': Mental health experiences of young autistic adults in England. *Autism*, *25*(3), 602–617.

22. Faraone, S. V., Asherson, P., Banaschewski, T., Biederman, J., Buitelaar, J. K., Ramos-Quiroga, J. A., ... & Franke, B. (2021). Attention-deficit/hyperactivity disorder. *Nature Reviews Disease Primers*, *7*, 47.

23. van den Heuvel, O. A., Boedhoe, P. S. W., Bertolín, S., Bruin, W. B., Francks, C., Ivanov, I., ... & Schmaal, L. (2022). Cortico-striato-thalamo-cortical circuits in OCD: A meta-analysis of structural and functional MRI studies. *Neuroscience & Biobehavioral Reviews*, 132, 1221–1237

24. Stein, D. J., Costa, D. L. C., Lochner, C., Miguel, E. C., Reddy, Y. C. J., Shavitt, R. G., ... & Fineberg, N. A. (2019). Obsessive–compulsive disorder. *Nature Reviews Disease Primers*, *5*(1), 52.

Touching Stones

1. Lee, J. L. C., Nader, K., & Schiller, D. (2017). An update on memory reconsolidation: Implications for therapy. *Nature Reviews Neuroscience, 18*(7), 336–351.

2. Hitchcock, C., Rees, C. S., & Dalgleish, T. (2017). The devil's in the detail: Accessibility of specific personal memories supports diagnostic differentiation of major depression. *Behaviour Research and Therapy, 97*, 113–121.

3. Hitchcock, C., Rees, C. S., & Dalgleish, T. (2017). The devil's in the detail: Accessibility of specific personal memories supports diagnostic differentiation of major depression. *Behaviour Research and Therapy, 97*, 113–121.

4. Hirst, W., Phelps, E. A., Meksin, R., Vaidya, C. J., Johnson, M. K., Mitchell, K. J., ... & Olsson, A. (2009). Long-term memory for the terrorist attack of September 11: Flashbulb memories, event memories, and the factors that influence their retention. *Journal of Experimental Psychology: General, 138*(2), 161–176.

Adolescence

1. Barsky, A. J., & Borus, J. F. (1999). Functional somatic syndromes. Annals of Internal Medicine, 130(11), 910–921.

2. American Psychiatric Association. (2022). Diagnostic and statistical manual of mental disorders (5th ed., text rev.).

3. American Psychiatric Association. (2022). *Diagnostic and statistical manual of mental disorders* (5th ed., text rev., pp. 316–319). American Psychiatric Publishing.

4. Salkovskis, P. M., & Warwick, H. M. (2001). Meaning, misinterpretations, and medicine: A cognitive-behavioral approach to understanding health anxiety and hypochondriasis. In G. Asmundson et al. (Eds.), Health anxiety: Clinical and research perspectives on hypochondriasis and related conditions (pp. 202–222). Wiley.

5. Garralda, M. E. (2010). Somatisation in children. Journal of the Royal Society of Medicine, 103(6), 219–222.

6. Olatunji, B. O., Cisler, J. M., & Tolin, D. F. (2015). Quality of life in the anxiety disorders: A meta-analytic review. Clinical Psychology Review, 28(2), 57–72.

7. Padilla-Walker, L. M., & Nelson, L. J. (2012). Black hawk down? Establishing helicopter parenting as a distinct construct from other forms of parental control during emerging adulthood. *Journal of Adolescence, 35*(5), 1177–1190.

Thought Crimes

1. Exner, J. E. (2003). *The Rorschach: A comprehensive system* (4th ed.). Wiley.

2. Wegner, D. M. (1994). *Ironic processes of mental control. Psychological Review, 101*(1), 34–52.

3. Freud, S. (1961). *The ego and the id* (J. Strachey, Trans.). W. W. Norton. (Original work published 1923)

4. Leue, A., Borchard, B., & Hoyer, J. (2004) *Mental disorders in a forensic sample of sexual offenders. European Psychiatry, 19*(3), 123–130.

5. Veale, D., Freeston, M., Krebs, G., & Heyman, I. (2009). Risk assessment and management in obsessive–compulsive disorder. *Advances in Psychiatric Treatment, 15*(3), 222–232.

6. American Psychiatric Association. (2022). *Diagnostic and statistical manual of mental disorders* (5th ed., text rev.).

7. Levy, A., Nachshon, D., & Carmi, A. (2002). Psychiatry and law. Yozmot Heiliger

8. Orne, M. T., Dinges, D. F., & Orne, E. C. (1984). On the differential diagnosis of multiple personality in the forensic context. *The International Journal of Clinical and Experimental Hypnosis, 32*(2), 118–169.

9. Schechter, H. (1989). *Deviant: The shocking true story of Ed Gein, the original "psycho".* Pocket Books.

Original Sins

1. Hitchens, C. (1995). *The missionary position: Mother Teresa in theory and practice.* Verso. Pg 9.

2. Hitchens, C. (1994). *Hell's angel: Mother Teresa* [Television documentary]. Channel 4.

3. Hitchens, C. (1995). *The missionary position: Mother Teresa in theory and practice.* Verso. Pg.11.

4. Hitchens, C. (1995). *The missionary position: Mother Teresa in theory and practice.* Verso. Pg.39.

5. Büyüköksüz, E. (2022). The cognitive behavioural therapy of an adolescent with sexual and religious obsessions: A case report. *Journal of Cognitive-Behavioral Psychotherapy and Research, 11*(1), 74–82.

6. Ozment, S. E. (1983). *The age of reform, 1250–1550: An intellectual and religious history of late medieval and Reformation Europe.* Yale University Press.

7. Dante Alighieri. (2003). *Inferno* (A. Mandelbaum, Trans.). Bantam Books. (Original work published ca. 1320)

8. Durling, R. M., & Martinez, R. L. (1996). *Inferno* (Dante Alighieri). Oxford University Press.

9. Hollander, R. (2000). *Dante: A life in works.* Yale University Press.

10. Bloom, H. (Ed.). (2005). *The seven deadly sins.* Infobase Publishing.

11. Catechism of the Catholic Church. (1994). Libreria Editrice Vaticana.

12. Neusner, J. (2004). *Sin: A history.* Brandeis University Press.

13. IslamOnline. (n.d.). *The Islamic Perspective of Sin.* Retrieved from https://islamonline.net/en/the-islamic-perspective-of-sin/

14. Rahula, W. (1974). *What the Buddha taught.* Grove Press.

15. Jacobs, S.-E., Thomas, W., & Lang, S. (1997). *Two-spirit people: Native American gender identity, sexuality, and spirituality.* University of Illinois Press.

16. Williams, C. A. (1999). *Roman homosexuality: Ideologies of masculinity in classical antiquity.* Oxford University Press.

17. Morford, M. P. O., Lenardon, R. J., & Sham, M. (2018). *Classical mythology* (11th ed.). Oxford University Press.

18. The Holy Bible, King James Version. (1769/2017). Thomas Nelson. (Original work published 1611)

19. Young, M. B. (2000). *King James and the history of homosexuality.* Haworth Press.

20. Booth, M. (2016). *Queer Bible hermeneutics and the legacy of King James*. In J. Hornbeck & M. Sweeney (Eds.), *Sex, Gender, and the Sacred: Reconfiguring Religion* (pp. 113–131). Routledge.

21. Young, J. E., Klosko, J. S., & Weishaar, M. E. (2003). *Schema therapy: A practitioner's guide*. Guilford Press.

Echo's Chamber

1. British Association of Aesthetic Plastic Surgeons. (2023). *Annual Audit Results 2022*. https://baaps.org.uk

2. Veale, D., Gledhill, L. J., Christodoulou, P., & Hodsoll, J. (2016). Body dysmorphic disorder in different settings: A systematic review and estimated weighted prevalence. *Body Image*, 18, 168–186.

3. Phillips, K. A., Hart, A. S., & Menard, W. (2017). Psychopathology and severity of body dysmorphic disorder in a multidisciplinary treatment setting. *Journal of Clinical Psychiatry*, 78(4), e370–e376.

4. Crerand, C. E., Franklin, M. E., & Sarwer, D. B. (2020). Body dysmorphic disorder and cosmetic surgery. *Plastic and Reconstructive Surgery*, 145(5), 1310–1316.

5. American Psychiatric Association. (2013). *Diagnostic and statistical manual of mental disorders* (5th ed.). Arlington, VA: American Psychiatric Publishing.

6. Crerand, C. E., Franklin, M. E., & Sarwer, D. B. (2007). Body dysmorphic disorder and cosmetic surgery. *Plastic and Reconstructive Surgery*, 120(7), 2097–2105.

7. Phillips, K. A., Grant, J., Siniscalchi, J., & Albertini, R. S. (2001). Surgical and nonpsychiatric medical treatment of patients with body dysmorphic disorder. *Psychosomatics*, 42(6), 504–510.

8. Phillips, K. A. (2005). *The broken mirror: Understanding and treating body dysmorphic disorder* (Rev. ed.). Oxford University Press.

9. Veale, D. (2004). Advances in a cognitive behavioural model of body dysmorphic disorder. *Body Image*, 1(1), 113–125.

10. Dyer, R. (1997). White: Essays on race and culture. Routledge.

11. Garland-Thomson, R. (2002). The politics of staring: Visual rhetorics of disability in popular photography. *Disability Studies Quarterly, 22*(2), 56–75.

12. Veale, D., & Neziroglu, F. (2010). *Body dysmorphic disorder: A treatment manual*. Wiley-Blackwell.

13. Kernberg, O. F. (1984). *Severe personality disorders: Psychotherapeutic strategies*. Yale University Press.

14. Rogers, C. R. (1959). A theory of therapy, personality and interpersonal relationships, as developed in the client-centered framework. In S. Koch (Ed.), *Psychology: A study of a science. Vol. 3: Formulations of the person and the social context* (pp. 184–256). McGraw-Hill.

15. Schneider, S. C., Turner, C. M., Mond, J., & Hudson, J. L. (2017). Prevalence and correlates of body dysmorphic disorder in a community sample of adolescents. *Australian & New Zealand Journal of Psychiatry*, 51(5), 479–485.

Avoiding Cracks

1. Freud, S. (1959). *Inhibitions, symptoms and anxiety*. In J. Strachey (Ed. & Trans.), *The standard edition of the complete psychological works of Sigmund Freud* (Vol. 20, pp. 75–174). London: Hogarth Press. (Original work published 1926)

2. Joseph, B. (1989). *Psychic equilibrium and psychic change: Selected papers of Betty Joseph*. London: Routledge

3. Fenichel, O. (1945). *The psychoanalytic theory of neurosis*. New York: W. W. Norton.

4. Freud, S. (1955). *Notes upon a case of obsessional neurosis* (Rat Man). In J. Strachey (Ed. & Trans.), *The standard edition of the complete psychological works of Sigmund Freud* (Vol. 10, pp. 151–318). London: Hogarth Press. (Original work published 1909)

5. Hayes, S. C., Wilson, K. G., Gifford, E. V., Follette, V. M., & Strosahl, K. (1996). Experiential avoidance and behavioral disorders: A functional dimensional approach to diagnosis and treatment. *Journal of Consulting and Clinical Psychology, 64*(6), 1152–1168.

6. Frederickson, J. (2018). *Co-creating change: Effective dynamic therapy techniques.* Seven Leaves Press.

7. Heimberg, R. G., Brozovich, F. A., & Rapee, R. M. (2010). A cognitive-behavioral model of social anxiety disorder: Update and extension. In S. G. Hofmann & P. M. DiBartolo (Eds.), *Social anxiety: Clinical, developmental, and social perspectives* (2nd ed., pp. 395–422). Elsevier.

8. Clark, D. M., & Wells, A. (1995). A cognitive model of social phobia. In R. G. Heimberg, M. R. Liebowitz, D. A. Hope, & F. R. Schneier (Eds.), *Social phobia: Diagnosis, assessment, and treatment* (pp. 69–93). Guilford Press.

9. Tangney, J. P., Stuewig, J., & Mashek, D. J. (2007). Moral emotions and moral behavior. *Annual Review of Psychology, 58*, 345–372.

10. Klein, M. (1935). *A contribution to the psychogenesis of manic-depressive states. International Journal of Psycho-Analysis, 16*, 145–174.

11. Klein, M. (1946). Notes on some schizoid mechanisms. International Journal of Psycho-Analysis, 27, 99–110.

12. Fonagy, P., & Bateman, A. (2006). Mechanisms of change in mentalization-based treatment of borderline personality disorder. Journal of Clinical Psychology, 62(4), 411—30.

13. Klein, M. (1997). Envy and gratitude and other works 1946–1963. London: Hogarth Press. (Original work published 1946)

14. Grice, T. A., Alcock, K., & Scior, K. (2018). Mental health disclosure among clinical psychologists in training: Perfectionism and pragmatism. *Clinical Psychology & Psychotherapy, 25*(5), 647–656.

Warheads

1. Shafran, R., Cooper, Z., & Fairburn, C. G. (2002). Clinical perfectionism: A cognitive–behavioural analysis. *Behaviour Research and Therapy, 40*(7), 773–791.

2. McWilliams, N. (2011). *Psychoanalytic diagnosis: Understanding personality structure in the clinical process* (2nd ed.). The Guilford Press.

3. McWilliams, N. (2011). *Psychoanalytic diagnosis: Understanding personality structure in the clinical process* (2nd ed., pp. 176–196). The Guilford Press.

4. Kernberg, O. F. (2004). *Aggressivity, narcissism, and self-destructiveness in the psychotherapeutic relationship.* Yale University Press.

5. Young, J. E., Klosko, J. S., & Weishaar, M. E. (2003). *Schema therapy: A practitioner's guide.* Guilford Press.

6. Saleh, S. A. (2022). Defense mechanisms and personality disorders. In *The Psychology of Consciousness: Theory and Practice* (pp. 61–79). Springer.

7. Young, J. E., Klosko, J. S., & Weishaar, M. E. (2003). *Schema therapy: A practitioner's guide.* Guilford Press.

Containment

1. Zeng, W., Huang, D., Li, Q., Xu, Y., Xu, Z., Wu, C., Chen, Z., & Yang, Y. (2022). The prevalence of moral injury and its association with mental health in healthcare workers during the COVID-19 pandemic: A systematic review and meta-analysis. *Archives of Public Health, 80,* 269.

2. Appelbom, S., Nordström, A., & Finnes, A. (2024). Healthcare worker burnout during a persistent crisis: A case–control study. *Occupational Medicine, 74*(4), 297–303.

3. Centers for Disease Control and Prevention (CDC). (2022). *Mental health of healthcare workers during the COVID-19 pandemic.* U.S. Department of Health and Human Services.

4. Siddiqui, M., Wadoo, O., Currie, J., Alabdulla, M., Reagu, S. M., & Muraoka, H. (2022). *The impact of COVID-19 pandemic on individuals with pre-existing obsessive-compulsive disorder in the State of Qatar: An exploratory cross-sectional study*. Frontiers in Psychiatry, 13, Article 833394.

5. Sifferlin, A. (2020, May 7). *For people with OCD, the COVID-19 pandemic is a nightmare come true*. TIME. https://time.com/5833482/ocd-coronavirus-pandemic/

6. Time. (2022, January 20). *Pandemic Anxiety Is Fueling OCD Symptoms—Even for People Without the Disorder*. *Time*. Retrieved from Time website: https://time.com/6140256/ocd-covid-19-anxiety/

7. Flett, G. L., & Hewitt, P. L. (2020). *The perfectionism pandemic meets COVID-19: Understanding the stress, distress and problems in living for perfectionists during the global health crisis*. *Journal of Concurrent Disorders, 2*(1), 80–105.

8. Ivandic, R., Kirchmaier, T., & Wettstein, D. (2021). Did the first COVID-19 lockdown reduce domestic abuse? *American Journal of Health Economics, 7*(3), 280–320.

9. Office for National Statistics. (2020). Crime in England and Wales: Year ending Mar 2021. *ONS*. Retrieved from https://www.ons.gov.uk 04th March 2025.

10. Bertram, F., Heinrich, F., Fröb, D., Wulff, B., Ondruschka, B., Püschel, K., König, H.-H., & Hajek, A. (2021). Loneliness among homeless individuals during the first wave of the COVID-19 pandemic. *International Journal of Environmental Research and Public Health, 18*(6), 3035.

11. Brennan, L., Lalonde, R. N., & Gaudreau, P. (2022). Perfectionistic self-presentation and coping during the COVID-19 pandemic: A double-edged sword. *Personality and Individual Differences, 185*, 111257.

12. Smith, M. M., Sherry, S. B., Rnic, K., Saklofske, D. H., Enns, M. W., & Gralnick, T. M. (2016). Are perfectionism dimensions risk factors for depressive symptoms after controlling for neuroticism? A meta-analysis of 10,741 participants. *European Journal of Personality, 30*(2), 201–212. https://doi.org/10.1002/per.2053

13. Flett, G. L., & Hewitt, P. L. (2020). The perfectionism pandemic meets COVID-19: Understanding the stress, distress, and problems in living for perfectionists during the global health crisis. *Journal of Concurrent Disorders*, *2*(1), 80–105.

14. Probst, T., Stippl, P., & Stigler, K. (2021). *Therapy via video conferencing: A meta-analysis comparing video and in-person psychotherapy outcomes during COVID-19*. *Journal of Affective Disorders*, 294, 97–104.

15. Roske, K., Marwitz, S. E., & Peters, M. L. (2024). Perceived benefits of reduced social demands during COVID-19: A mixed-method study of introversion and mental wellbeing. *International Journal of Psychology*, *59*(1), 23–34.

16. Preti, E., Di Pierro, R., Fanti, E., Madeddu, F., & Calati, R. (2020). Personality disorders in time of pandemic. *Current Psychiatry Reports*, *22*(12), 80.

17. Dipnall, J. F., Pasco, J. A., Williams, L. J., & Berk, M. (2024). The long shadow of isolation: Effects of prolonged social distancing on perfectionism and anxiety. *Journal of Affective Disorders*, *337*, 65–72.

18. Gilmartin, T. J., Lane, T. J., & Hawes, D. J. (2024). Socially prescribed perfectionism and mental health during COVID-19 lockdown: The mediating role of emotional regulation. *Personality and Individual Differences*, *207*, 112126.

19. Benatti, B., Albert, U., Maina, G., Battaglia, F., Bramante, S., & Fagiolini, A. (2020). What happened to patients with obsessive compulsive disorder during the COVID-19 pandemic? A multicentre report from tertiary clinics in Northern Italy. *Frontiers in Psychiatry, 11*, 720.

20. Flett, G. L., & Hewitt, P. L. (2022). Perfectionism in the time of COVID-19: Exploring the mechanisms that may explain why perfectionists are vulnerable to distress in a global pandemic. *Journal of Rational-Emotive & Cognitive-Behavior Therapy, 40*(1), 59–83.

Unusual Suspects

1. Shapiro, F. (2018). *Eye movement desensitization and reprocessing (EMDR) therapy: Basic principles, protocols, and procedures* (3rd ed.). The Guilford Press.

2. Nazari, H., Momeni, F., Jariani, M., & Tarrahi, M. J. (2011). Comparison of eye movement desensitisation and reprocessing and citalopram in treatment of obsessive-compulsive disorder. *International Journal of Psychiatry in Clinical Practice, 15*(4), 270–274.

3. Marr, J. (2012). Eye movement desensitisation and reprocessing (EMDR) in the treatment of obsessive-compulsive disorder. *British Journal of Guidance & Counselling, 40*(3), 255–261.

4. Triscari, M. T., Faraci, P., D'Angelo, V., Urso, A., & Vetri, L. (2015). Effectiveness of EMDR in OCD: A case series. *Journal of EMDR Practice and Research, 9*(3), 136–149.

5. Rogers, C. R. (1951). *Client-centered therapy: Its current practice, implications and theory*. Boston: Houghton Mifflin.

New Blood

1. Russell, E. J., Fawcett, J. M., & Mazmanian, D. (2013). Risk of obsessive-compulsive disorder in pregnant and postpartum women: A meta-analysis. *Journal of Clinical Psychiatry, 74*(4), 377–385.

2. Pellegrini, L., Favaro, A., & Tenconi, E. (2022). Suicidal behaviour in obsessive-compulsive disorder: A systematic review. *Journal of Affective Disorders, 296*, 346–357.

3. Volkova, E., Hadj-Moussa, S., & Dempsey, C. (2021). Initial evidence for symptoms of postpartum relationship-focused obsessive-compulsive disorder and their impact on parent–infant interactions. *Frontiers in Psychiatry, 12*, 589949.

4. Cassidy, J., & Shaver, P. R. (Eds.). (2016). *Handbook of attachment: Theory, research, and clinical applications* (3rd ed.). Guilford Press.

Precious Things

1. Wikipedia contributors. (2024, May 13). *Edmund Trebus*. Wikipedia. https://en.wikipedia.org/wiki/Edmund_Trebus

2. BBC. (1999). *A Life of Grime* [Television series]. BBC Two.

3. Boseley, S. (2002, October 5). Edmund Trebus. *The Guardian*.

4. All biographical details about Mr Edmund Trebus have been sourced from publicly available media, including *The Guardian*, *Wikipedia*, *The Telegraph*, and news archives. No clinical data or private records were used. Any commentary reflects public knowledge and should not be interpreted as diagnostic.

5. Tolin, D. F., Frost, R. O., Steketee, G., Gray, K. D., & Fitch, K. E. (2008). The economic and social burden of compulsive hoarding. *Psychiatry Research, 160*(2), 200–211.

6. Winnicott, D. W. (1953). Transitional objects and transitional phenomena. *International Journal of Psycho-Analysis, 34*, 89–97.

7. Frost, R. O., & Steketee, G. (2010). *Stuff: Compulsive hoarding and the meaning of things*. New York: Houghton Mifflin Harcourt.

8. Laidlaw, K., & Pachana, N. A. (2009). *Cognitive behaviour therapy with older people: Innovations across care settings*. Wiley-Blackwell.

9. Viswanathan, A., & Rao, N. P. (2020). Late-onset obsessive-compulsive disorder: A review. *Frontiers in Psychiatry, 11*, 554.

10. Ayers, C. R., Saxena, S., Golshan, S., & Wetherell, J. L. (2014). Age at onset and clinical features of late life compulsive hoarding. *International Journal of Geriatric Psychiatry, 25*(2), 142–149.

11. Thew, G. R., & Salkovskis, P. M. (2016). Cognitive behaviour therapy for hoarding disorder. *Cognitive and Behavioral Practice, 23*(2), 204–218.

12. Grisham, J. R., & Baldwin, P. A. (2015). Neuropsychological and neurophysiological insights into hoarding disorder. *Neuropsychiatric Disease and Treatment, 11*, 951–962.

13. Tolin, D. F., Frost, R. O., Steketee, G., Gray, K. D., & Fitch, K. E. (2008). The economic and social burden of compulsive hoarding. *Psychiatry Research, 160*(2), 200–211.

14. Dozier, M. E., Ayers, C. R., & Whitfield, E. L. (2016). The role of trauma and stressful life events among individuals with hoarding disorder. *Journal of Nervous and Mental Disease, 204*(6), 471–476.

15. Li, L., Wang, Y., & Zhang, X. (2023). Has the UK Campaign to End Loneliness reduced loneliness and improved mental health in older age? A difference-in-differences design. *ResearchGate*. https://www.researchgate.net/publication/374853391

16. Overend, K., Bosanquet, K., Bailey, D., Foster, D., Gascoyne, S., Lewis, H., ... & Chew-Graham, C. (2015). Revealing hidden depression in older people: A qualitative study within a randomised controlled trial. *BMC Family Practice, 16*(1), 142.

17. Tolin, D. F., Frost, R. O., & Steketee, G. (2015). *Hoarding disorder: Recognition, assessment and treatment*. The Cognitive Behaviour Therapist, 8, E1.

18. Department for Constitutional Affairs. (2007). *Mental Capacity Act 2005 Code of Practice*. The Stationery Office.

19. Sturge, C., & Clare, I. C. H. (2005). Clinical and ethical issues in the assessment of capacity. *Clinical Psychology Review, 25*(7), 954–975.

20. UK Government. (1990). *Environmental Protection Act 1990*. London: Her Majesty's Stationery Office. Retrieved from https://www.legislation.gov.uk/ukpga/1990/43

21. Greater Poland Uprising. (n.d.). *Wikipedia*. Retrieved March 16, 2025, from https://en.wikipedia.org/wiki/Greater_Poland_uprising

22. Encyclopedia Britannica. (n.d.). *Treaty of Versailles*. Retrieved March 16, 2025, from https://www.britannica.com/event/Treaty-of-Versailles-1919

23. The Guardian. (2002, October 5). *Edmund Trebus*. https://www.theguardian.com/news/2002/oct/05/guardianobituaries

24. Nawrocki, T., & Bierwiaczonek, K. (2019). Survival and Trauma. The Collective Memory of the World War II in a Silesian Village.

25. Military Wiki. (n.d.). *Edmund Trebus*. Retrieved March 16, 2025, from https://military-history.fandom.com/wiki/Edmund_Trebus

26. WW2 in Color. (n.d.). *Polish troops at Monte Cassino*. Retrieved March 16, 2025, from https://www.ww2incolor.com/gallery/polish-forces/19929/polish-troops-at-monte-cassino

27. The Telegraph. (2002, October 3). *Edmund Trebus*. https://www.telegraph.co.uk/news/obituaries/1409049/Edmund-Trebus.html

28. Wikipedia. (n.d.-a). *Edmund Trebus*. Retrieved March 16, 2025, from https://en.wikipedia.org/wiki/Edmund_Trebus

29. Staff, D. (2002, October 5). Edmund Trebus. *The Guardian*. https://www.theguardian.com/news/2002/oct/05/guardianobituaries

Drawing Circles

1. Christ, G. H. (2000). Healing children's grief: Surviving a parent's death from cancer. Oxford University Press.

2. Slaughter, V., & Griffiths, M. (2007). Death understanding and fear of death in young children. *Clinical Child Psychology and Psychiatry*, 12(4), 525–535.

3. Bowlby, J. (1980). *Attachment and loss: Vol. 3. Loss: Sadness and depression*. New York: Basic Books.

4. Freud, S. (1957). *Thoughts for the times on war and death*. In J. Strachey (Ed. & Trans.), *The standard edition of the complete psychological works of Sigmund Freud* (Vol. 14, pp. 275–300). London: Hogarth Press. (Original work published 1915)

5. Becker, E. (1973). *The denial of death*. New York: Free Press.

6.

7. Tonkin, L. (1996). Growing around grief: Another way of looking at grief and recovery. *Bereavement Care*, 15(1), 10.

8. Steinhauser, K. E., Christakis, N. A., Clipp, E. C., McNeilly, M., McIntyre, L., & Tulsky, J. A. (2000). *Factors considered important at the end of life by patients, family, physicians, and other care providers.* JAMA, 284(19), 2476–2482.

9. Ware, B. (2012). *The top five regrets of the dying: A life transformed by the dearly departing.* Hay House.

10. Roncero, M., Belloch, A., & Perpiñá, C. (2023). *Obsessive-compulsive personality disorder and the end of life: A systematic review of psychological outcomes and clinical implications.* Clinical Psychology Review, 99, 102233.

Leveraging Life

1. Petersen, W. (Director). (1984). *The NeverEnding Story* [Film]. Bavaria Film; Neue Constantin Film.

2. Schwartz, R. C. (1995). *Internal family systems therapy.* Guilford Press.

3. Schwartz, R. C. (2021). *No bad parts: Healing trauma and restoring wholeness with the Internal Family Systems model.* Sounds True.

About the Author

Dr. James Spiers is a British psychologist and EMDR practitioner with extensive clinical experience in the field of mental health. He is a chartered member and associate fellow of the British Psychological Society, and registered as a Counselling Psychologist with the Health and Care Professions Council (HCPC) in England.

A HANDY GUIDE TO

NON EPILEPTIC ATTACK DISORDER

Living with Dissociative Seizures

DR JAMES SPIERS

Practiceebooks.com

Other Titles by the Author

COMPULSIVE
OBSESSIVE PEOPLE

DR JAMES SPIERS

Printed in Great Britain
by Amazon